emotional intimacy

overlooked requirement for survival

Alan M. Dahms

Library of Congress Card Catalog Number 72-78443
ISBN:0-87108-184-9

"Faculty Club" and "Professor Emeritus" reprinted from *Colonel Johnson's Ride* by Robert Huff by permission of the Wayne State University Press.
© Copyright 1959 Wayne State University Press Detroit 2, Michigan. All rights reserved

Pruett Publishing Company
Boulder, Colorado 80302
Printed in the United States of America

Particular mention is due to Bob Huff and the Wayne State University Press for permission to reprint "Faculty Club" and "Professor Emeritus" from *Colonel Johnson's Ride.* Grateful acknowledgment is also made to George Drew (Hudson Valley Community College) and Donald Decker (University of Northern Colorado) for their poems, and to Susie Irby for her interesting drawings.

preface

The desire to write down my thoughts about emotional intimacy springs from seemingly unrelated experiences. During recent years I have worked in retail business, as a medical researcher in a college of medicine, as a real estate executive, and most recently as a university instructor in the field of psychology.

In some major ways, I have challenged the American Dream, which prescribes high school, college, graduate school, marriage, mortgage, and 2.3 children—*necessarily* in that order. Following graduation with a bachelor's degree in psychology, sociology, and chemistry in 1960, the completion of some coursework in medical school, and service in the military, I pursued three different occupations in a six-year period.

First, I worked in the retail tire and rubber business in San Francisco while auditing courses in philosophy offered by universities in that area. Next, I worked as part of a research team in the department of pharmacology at a western university's school of medicine.

We pursued research related to organ transplants, auto-immune diseases, and population control. I then joined the staff of a real estate and investment company with offices in five western states; I still serve as an executive vice-president of that firm.

I was twenty-eight years old when my interests focused on graduate work in psychology. At long last it seemed that I was deciding what I wanted to be when I grew up!

For three years, since completion of my graduate work, I have been a therapist, classroom instructor, and consultant in the area of human growth and development. The promising growth-group or sensitivity group movement has intrigued me; and my experiences as a group leader, in a variety of settings, are incorporated in what follows.

I have grown weary of factions attempting to impose their "truth" on others. Such pressures abound within academic departments, business circles, and on research teams.

The many books and the men who proclaim the need for human love also distress me. The message too often seems to be, "If you are a good person, you will care for your fellow man." The "Sunday only" Christian and the ambivalent group member behaviorally illustrate this message.

The thesis of this book is that an enlightened commitment to constructive human relationships at all levels of the social system is not a sentimental preoccupation. It is an overlooked requirement for individual and collective survival which is as essential to life as food, water, and sleep. Without some degree of emotional intimacy, we will kill each other. Tragically, we seem to need a "reason" to reach out to each other. *Survival* is a good reason.

It is hoped that not only professionals but also lay helpers, volunteers, and process-oriented persons in various settings will find that the ideas advanced here prod them to consider their human relationships in broader perspective.

I offer myself and my thoughts without any pompous proclamation that I have *the* answer. I delight in the opportunity to expose my fellow travelers to ideas that have become meaningful to me. Any attempt on my part to determine which ideas came from where, or how they were influenced by other ideas, seems doomed to certain failure. Part I is a consideration of emotional intimacy as a working hypothesis; a series of models is found in Part II; Part III contains thoughts on possible future directions in light of my definition of a psychologically defined mutual "good." A list of references is offered at the end of the book for those interested in further reading.

The ideas in this book, although tempered by extensive reading in literature and behavioral science, have been most influenced by those relationships within which I enjoyed some degree of emotional intimacy. Professor O. J. Harvey at the University of Colorado, Provost Donald Decker, and Professors Arno Luker, Richard Usher, Bud Halldorson, and Claire Quinlan at the University of Northern Colorado, Professors Arthur Combs, Sidney Jourard, W. Edgar Moore, Bradley Fisher, and James Pitts at the University of Florida, Professor Vernie Iazzetta at Metropolitan State College, Denver, and Harold E. Parker, A.C.S.W., Fort Logan Mental Health Center, have all exerted profound influence on my current view. I am sure that they would agree that my gratitude to them will be best demonstrated if the ideas expressed here somehow encourage others to consider the necessity for evolving, maintaining, and enhancing emotionally intimate relationships.

I am also indebted to those students, clients, and growth-group colleagues who have invited me into their worlds and have demonstrated so movingly the magnificence and coping capacities of all men. Our mutual experiences have helped to consolidate the ideas in this book. Gale Namie Dupuis, Jack Storne, Wilson Mastry, Kamaldeen Ibraheem, Tay Tanya, and Devra Zinn gave me special help.

A special thank you, too, to those people, beginning with my parents, who taught me about emotional intimacy, and to Pollard Talton for her help in typing the manuscript.

I am grateful to Alice Levine for her thorough editing of the final manuscript.

Alan M. Dahms

Denver, Colorado
May, 1972

contents

WALT WHITMAN IN THE ZOO

I

Surrounded by all the animals,
The peaceful creatures he had loved,
The poet, like a good gray ghost,
Hovers here,
Colossal as the land he revered,
Looking out
Across a various continent,
The map of his interior.

II

This poet, gazing with a bronze
Look at the copper land, appears
Still ready for the Open Road,
Not knowing how
We have destroyed the destiny
That he had thought so manifest.
Manifest! How clever of Walt
To advertize himself and not
America!
He sensed the safety in Myself
And shouted it loudly everyday,
Using for symbol a restless land
Peopled by replicas of himself;
And his interior stayed rich,
Even as the yellowing map
Cracked apart,
Leaving a gravely rusted dream
Haunted by spectres of ourselves.

III

Sounds of the animals fill the air
And seem to hum about Walt's head
As he admits,
"Yes, I am happy that you found
Me out; I wanted you to know."
His features seem
To wrinkle into a crocodile grin,
And I abandon him to the zoo.

—George Drew

part I
intimacy reconsidered
introduction

Conflict and alienation seem to be the ever-present and unavoidable by-products of the rapid changes in man's society. Today's conflicts exist between student and university, black and white, longhair and hard-hat, young and old, rich and poor, and among nations. Dissidents are using extreme methods to obtain unconditional physical and psychological surrender from those in power. Those in power must resort to equal measures to maintain their position.

The continuation of human life at a level acceptable to fully functioning men seems to be in doubt. It is the thesis of this book that an increased commitment to the facilitation and practice of emotional intimacy— from the conjugal to the international level—is not a sentimental preoccupation; it is nothing less than a somewhat overlooked *survival requirement.*

What is emotional intimacy? What relation does it have to our survival and the quality of our lives? How can one tell if a capacity for intimacy exists? How does one develop that capacity?

A dedication to understanding some of the dimensions of humanness as defined in humanistic psychology is not posited as *the* simplistic answer to major dilemmas of modern man, but as an emphasis that has not been adequately explored. This commitment to maximize the human qualities that unite us emphasizes methods of freeing the individual and rests squarely on a deep faith in the positive nature of the growth processes in man. This view is somewhat incompatible with certain aspects of more traditional approaches which imply that man's instincts must often be controlled.

If the reader discovers personal meaning in some of the ideas in this book and begins an examination of his assumptions about human behavior, the book will have served a useful purpose.

1

need for intimacy

One of the most critical environmental factors in human development seems to be physical contact with a loving individual. Experimental work by René Spitz and Harry Harlow indicate that physical and emotional impairment can result from the absence of physical intimacy.

If, during the first five or six years of a child's life, the mother-child relationship is deficient, permanent physical, social, and emotional impairment can result. René Spitz studied children who were institutionalized. He compared children who had been nursed by their mothers to children who were cared for, in groups of 8 to 12, by a nurse. While the youngsters whose mothers were available showed normal development, 37 percent of the other children died during the same period. A great majority of the remainder of the deprived group were negatively affected for life, either physically or mentally or both.

Harry Harlow's studies in the Primate Laboratory at the University of Wisconsin revealed that young monkeys expressed a preference for a terry-cloth, monkey-like substitute mother over a wire mesh equivalent. They clung to the terry-cloth "mother" even when feeding from the wire one. When faced with an unfamiliar object, the monkeys ran to the terry-cloth "mother" for protection. There seemed to be something about the terry-cloth mother that provided the monkeys with comfort and a feeling of security. Later studies by Harlow indicated that monkeys raised by mechanical "mothers" demonstrated symptoms of maladjustment: they were aggressive, unfriendly, and sexually incompetent.

The work that has been done with infants between the ages of six and nine months seems to indicate that the loss of a well-defined love object at this age can literally be a fatal tragedy. When the mother object is removed through death or illness, infants often regress physically and become unresponsive to their environment. Often, all attempts to substitute another love object are fruitless and the infant dies.

The need for human closeness has also been explored from a sociological perspective. Erich Fromm, Eric Hoffer, and Marshall McLuhan have dealt with this topic.

Erich Fromm's works, beginning with *Escape From Freedom* (1941), maintain that few persons have developed the capacity to cope effectively with freedom from familiar primary ties to family, church, and social structures. In times of change, people seem to organize in groups for a feeling of belonging. For example, when medieval society began to crumble and factories emerged, the Reformation seemed to provide a cause that furnished a new sense of belonging. In Germany, in the 1920's, the collapse of the monarchy was followed by rampant inflation; the society was in rapid flux and many felt the need to join a cause for a new sense of identity. Tragically, the cause was the National Socialist Party's drive for power, which exerted such a profound influence on the course of human progress in the twentieth century.

Fromm deftly points out the similarities between these two situations and conditions in the United States since 1941. There have been some rapid changes in family and church ties; that is, in the sources of primary psychological ties. He maintains that in this situation the two main escape mechanisms that were used in the two previous instances are still being utilized. People conform either by joining a cause or embracing a spirit of destructiveness. He posited the creative expression of personality through love and work as the desired solution to the feeling of alienation and lack of ties. He further pointed out this creative love and work alternative is psychologically available to too few. It would seem from his statements that the desire to belong, the desire to be intimate, is so strong that it can impel us into destruction unless we find other alternatives.

Eric Hoffer pointed out in *The True Believer* that when a society is in rapid flux many persons will embrace any cause, as "true believers," in a desperate attempt to regain the psychological identity. It does not matter what the cause is. It may be Hitler's Youth Corps, Christianity, communism, the ecology movement, alternative life styles, or politics. Hoffer agrees with Fromm that constructive love and work alternatives are too seldom chosen when people are faced with a loss of primary ties.

Marshall McLuhan, a controversial prophet of a new electronic age of communication, has documented our present isolation. He has pointed out that primitive tribal man was forced to rely on all his sensory equipment in order to avoid danger and capture food. Survival information was passed verbally. Following the invention of the printing press, however, man's primary means of communication became non-verbal. During this period, those members of the society who were able to read and write were greatly rewarded, and a man's worth to a society was defined in these terms. One result of this new era was a sense of isolation. Men were forced to compete on intellectual terms for the highest rewards the social order had to offer. The relative isolation and encapsulation of the next 500 years may have incapacitated us in terms of relating productively and fully with one another.

McLuhan contends that the world tribe that has been emerging since Marconi's invention of the telegraph, has come of age with the electronic revolution. Two billion people could have watched Astronaut Neil Armstrong put his foot on the moon in 1969 if they had made an effort to be close to a television set. In this new era, the world tribe—the entire population of the planet—can witness an event that takes place on another planet, just as primitive man watched their tribe members bring fish back to the village.

So, despite our far-reaching network of communications and our ability to share events, our sense of isolation is growing. Perhaps we have been crippled by 500 years of alienation and are unable to relate fully and openly with each other. We may have some unlearning and relearning to do in order to participate fully in the "Town Meetings of the World."

In order to reach each other, we must begin to unlearn some of the "oughts" and "shoulds" that we live by. Many American rules were founded originally on Puritan premises. Our Puritan-based ethics tell us to withhold ourselves, to live ascetically, to mistrust others (they may be the devil in disguise!), and to throw all our energy into competitive work. Before we can regain our capacity for intimacy we need to unlearn some of these rules and learn to relate rather than withdraw. Our psychological and physical survival depend on it.

The risks of evolving and maintaining intimacy are worth taking. To the degree that we encourage interpersonal distance instead of intimacy, we seem to create conditions for interpersonal and intergroup conflict. When we see others as different, distant, strange—as "not me," we find it much easier to harm them. Examples from diverse sources may serve to illustrate this point.

In his book *On Aggression*, Konrad Lorenz points out that species tend to instinctively resist the impulse to destroy another species as the other species becomes closer on the phylogenetic scale. One could illustrate this by saying that most human beings could kill a frog, fewer could kill a kitten, fewer still a puppy, and almost no one could easily kill a human infant, especially if the killing was to be accomplished with one's bare hands.

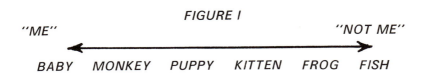

FIGURE I

"ME"   "NOT ME"

BABY   MONKEY   PUPPY   KITTEN   FROG   FISH

A similar dimension could be proposed *within* the human family. When hard-hats define longhairs as "not me" (as "fish"), it becomes easier to attack them. The same principle applies to black and white, old and young, and all other in-group-out-group conflicts.

Albert Speer, the master architect in Hitler's Third Reich, commented on the "not-me" concept in his memoirs, *Inside The Third Reich.* He contended that once a group within a larger group was singled out for "not me" status, not only were crimes against that group feasible, they were inevitable.

It is also possible for an individual to see *himself* as "not me." Such a phenomenon may be related to a lack of intimacy with others. Self-directed aggression has been observed in rhesus monkeys raised in social isolation. Based on his work in the Primate Laboratory at the University of Wisconsin, Harry Harlow has reported that self-aggressive behavior becomes prominent after the isolated monkey reaches 3 years of age and is frequently exhibited when strangers are present in the colony room. The angry, isolated monkeys chew on their own hands, arms, feet, or legs, sometimes to the point of tearing the flesh. Harlow notes that this behavior is somewhat similar to the self-destructive behavior displayed by autistic children. Self-aggression in humans can, of course, take the extreme form of suicide. It is common knowledge that single, widowed, or divorced people have more suicidal tendencies than married persons.

In a lighter vein, the "not me" concept is well illustrated in the science fiction, creature-feature movies. Bela Lugosi, Boris Karloff, Lon Chaney, and other great stars often portrayed a "not me" monster. In most of these works the victim becomes a monster through an accidental dose of a supposedly harmless liquid, an imprudent injection, or a mechanical mishap. He then spends the rest of the story struggling for love and understanding against the hostility shown him by others due to his physical transformation. Indeed, it seems the monster is often much *more* warm, gentle, and understanding than the scientists and citizens who oppose him! There is no need to reach very far to see the analogy between the difficulties of the science-fiction "monsters" and the difficulties of handicapped persons in our present society!

In his book, *Betrayal of the Body*, practicing psychoanalyst Alexander Lowen speaks about monsters. He observed that in every case he had seen in which the appearance of a person could be characterized as physically monstrous, the inner personality was that of an innocent child. Conversely, truly demonic (evil) persons often wear the outer aspect of sweetness and light. The devil hides under an angelic demeanor while the child hides behind the monster. His observations further underscore the dangers involved in assuming "monsters" are "not me."

Nilsson, a popular American songwriter and recording artist, explored the "me-not me" continuum in his recent album *The Point*. In the Land of Point everything was pointed—houses, farms, even people's heads. One young citizen, Oblio, was round-headed and was the target of derisive laughter and taunts from people with pointed heads. Even his pointed cap didn't stifle their objections to him. His "not me-ness" led to his banishment to the Pointless Forest with his dog Arrow who had been accused of complicity in the pointless matter. Since all things in the Land of Point must have points and he did not, he was forced to leave. Eventually he made his way back to the Land of Point and was received as a hero. He was the first person to return from the Pointless Forest. Oblio said, "Since everything has a point, even in the Pointless Forest, I must have a point!" "You have a point there," the citizens replied. All ended happily in the story. Often, all does *not* end happily for those humans banished from mainstream society because they can be called "not me."

Rhetorical devices are commonly used to set up "not me" categories of persons and things. A popular technique is to set up "god" terms (democratic, progressive, white) and "devil" terms (Communist, hippie) when trying to persuade someone of the inherent goodness of a cause. Politicians bent on supporting legislation against war call their opponents hawks. Freaks call peace officers pigs. Peace officers call minority citizens frogs. American soldiers in Viet Nam refer to the North Vietnamese as gooks. Hitler selected the Jew as his "international devil." Such distortions do not always result in interpersonal war.

Yet they may, since they fill our communications media. Although ostensibly harmless they recall Ambrose Bierce's definition of war: "A by-product of the arts of peace."

Traditional military training has as one of its goals the creation of "not me" status of the enemy. The enemy is referred to as gook, jap, commie, red, kraut, hippie, or frog. The assumption is, of course, that it is easier for a soldier to destroy an enemy he perceives as "not me." (Electronic technology has made this sort of indoctrination superfluous; ICBM warfare can be carried out by enemies who never even see each other.) Military uniforms also help to separate friend from foe. Even *within* one armed force, interpersonal distance is encouraged by the elaborate status designations broadcast by uniforms. Two persons designated by their uniforms as generals relate initially in very different ways than would either general if he were in the presence of a private. The first relationship is based on the recognition of a "me," while the second is based on "not me."

The dynamics of forcible rape seem related to the "me-not me" idea. Research indicates that the rapist is not usually the dark stranger in the trench coat as portrayed in entertainment media. Rather he is someone known by the victim, often a neighbor, relative, or friend. It seems that the victim extends powerful invitations to the rapist and when she wishes to halt his advances, she is unable to do so. Rape, like most other forms of human violation, may often require some degree of cooperation from the victim! She could have definitely stopped the situation if she had resisted actively rather than passively.

Studies on sexually aggressive (insistence short of brute force) college males shows that the rapist definitely sees the victim as "not me." Several variables seem present in such relationships:

1. The aggressive male sees his female target as undesirable and/or unavailable as a marriage prospect.
2. He distrusts women, including his mother, and has experienced a variety of heterosexual disappointments.
3. He is different from his victim in terms of socioeconomic and ethnic origins.

These studies support the comments of Konrad Lorenz and Albert Speer that as we see others as "not me," we are more likely to do them intellectual, physical, or emotional violence.

Several recent developments in the field of law enforcement show that there *are* ways to decrease "not me" tendencies, and thus increase intimacy.

Ghetto residents' preference for a minority police officer may be related to the perception of such an officer as more "me" than "not me."

In 1969, the Menlo Park Police Department of Menlo Park, California, introduced a new soft-look uniform, that was more like the street clothes of the typical citizen than a peace officer's uniform. The general results of a six-month study of that department's activities revealed that concern about safety, authority, and identification of a police officer in the soft-look uniform were not warranted. The department generally found itself more effective.

When the City of Lakewood, Colorado, was incorporated in 1969, the "police department" was called the Lakewood Department of Public Safety. The choice of Department of Public Safety as an organization name demonstrates a recognition of the need for "me" relationships with residents of the area. From the beginning, the department, which serves a rapidly growing suburban Denver area of 104,000 middle- to upper-class residents, adopted the soft-look style. Their attire parallels that of the professional businessman: dark blue blazers, light blue slacks, shirt, and a tie. There are no external metallic badges or signs of rank. Mr. Jack Storne, an agent with the Lakewood Department of Public Safety stated, "the soft look is particularly helpful when dealing with emotionally-charged situations such as domestic conflict and in dealing with children. The agent is not perceived as an authority threat by delinquents, dependents, and children in need of supervision. The soft look seems to help the agent achieve a 'me' status. People relate personally with the agent and have less tendency to oppose the agent physically."

Although the soft look can be a hazard in situations such as directing traffic and in fire and crowd control when the visibility of the traditional uniform is important, most agents are pleased with the present dress style.

Various agents report that the soft look influences not only the public, but also the agents in their approach to their responsibilities. The soft look seems to mellow and soften the agent's approach to citizens. He tends to be more democratic, less dictatorial, and understanding; perhaps citizens perceive him as "me" more easily and they expect a person-person rather than a cop-crook relationship. Psychologically, both agent and citizen tend to move toward a shared perception of their common concerns rather than their visually broadcast differences, as is often the case with traditional, metal-covered police uniforms.

Two recent surveys carried out by the department's Research and Development Division revealed highly favorable and receptive citizen attitudes toward the department. The surveys were conducted in May 1970 and 1971 (See Table 1). The studies used 455 randomly selected

TABLE 1

Evaluation of Service	May 1970	May 1971
Excellent	4%	11%
Good	28%	50%
Fair	31%	23.5%
Poor	14%	3.5%

citizens which represented .5% of the city's population. A statistically significant increase in satisfaction with the department's services was revealed.

In other law enforcement departments around the country, attempts are being made to close the "me-not me" distance. In Sausalito, California, the Police Department recently held encounter sessions between officers and psychiatrists during which they worked toward a deeper understanding of differences in minority cultures. A less authoritarian, role-oriented peace officer was a primary goal of this program.

An impressive laboratory experiment carried out at Yale University revealed that increased intimacy tended to reduce the willingness of subjects to administer punishment to others. Stanley Milgram found that subjects cooperating in a study of the effect of punishment on learning were astonishingly obedient. In this study, obedience was defined as complying with the experimenter's directions and continuing to administer high-voltage shock of increasing levels to a learner (collaborator of the experimenter). In a number of replications of the study, some 26 of the 40 volunteer subjects were completely obedient, even when hearing the protests of their victims! The *only* manipulated variable that dramatically *reduced* the tendency to hurt the learner-victim was that of physical proximity, which in the studies included face-to-face verbal interaction between subject and learner-victim. As the learner was brought physically closer, a decrement was observed in the subject's willingness to inflict punishment. As the distance decreased, a certain sense of community in terms of physical intimacy was formed, making it more difficult to hurt the learner. In this case, a sense of intimacy was a matter of survival to the learner-victim. Milgram's study suggests that if police officers and citizens can see each other as "me," there will be a decrease in willingness to inflict unwarranted harm on suspected offenders and on officers.

Aggression toward others may be the result of an intimacy deficiency in emotional relationships. As the studies of Spitz and Harlow show, such a lack in the early stages of life exerts a profound and long-lasting influence on later behavior.

There is an almost limitless number of ways to classify people from a psychological point of view; each classification is based on a theoretical model. One of the most intriguing theories has emerged from the field of social psychology. Research psychologists O. J. Harvey, David Hunt, and Harry Schroder, in their book *Conceptual Systems and Personality Organization*, assert that people demonstrate four qualitatively different styles of relating to the world in a relatively consistent fashion. Several thousand subjects have been studied in terms of conceptual system theory.

The first of these modal styles, System 1, is shown by some 30 percent of the subjects and is characterized by a low level of abstraction and a positive orientation toward authority figures. This style of relating to the world may be illustrated by the phrase, "Tell me what to do." It is vital for persons functioning within this conceptual orientation to know the rules and to abide by them. They relate comfortably to authority figures and to prescribed rules and regulations. They are capable of emotionally intimate ties with others. The authoritarian personality belongs to System 1.

The second style, System 2, is more abstract than System 1 and is oriented toward opposing the same extrapersonal referents. This style of functioning may be illustrated by the phrase, "Don't tell me what to do; I'll do what I want!" System 2 persons reject and oppose authority and external constraints; they do not comfortably relate to authority figures and prescribed rules and regulations. They are very distrustful and are very unwilling to expose their internal worlds. Interestingly, studies of delinquents and convicted felons show that the greatest amount of anti-social behavior and crime has been associated with System 2 persons. An example of this style, represented by some 15 percent of the population, is the student who is opposed to all institutional forms of education. He often seems to be a professional in negativism and cynicism. Nothing pleases him. He says, "The only solution to problems in education is to close the schools!" He is the rebel without a cause. He is against everything and for nothing. He seems to demonstrate the mode of destruction discussed by Fromm.

System 3 functioning is more abstract than in Systems 1 and 2 and is characterized by a positive orientation toward peer group authority and peer reference groups. System 3 functioning is oriented toward establishing and maintaining intragroup consensus as a step toward dependence and control of other people. This style of relating may be illustrated by the phrase, "What do all of you think I should do?" Persons operating in this system may place an inordinate emphasis on emotional intimacy and may use it in destructive ways. They are the manipulation artists. The "organization man," the man in the gray flannel suit, the man who gains his identity solely through his interpersonal and group identification illustrates System 3 functioning. Willy Loman in Arthur Miller's *Death of a Salesman*, for example, gained his feelings of worth from his employment as a salesman. Willy was steeped in the go-getter gospel with its goals of material success. At 60 he lived on reminiscences of past successes he'd had during his 34 years as a salesman. Although fired from his position, he would continue to say, "They really *do* like me upstate . . ." When his ties to his firm were cut he was unable to cope with new circumstances. Hence the title, *Death of a Salesman.* Some 20 percent of the population seems to fall within System 3.

System 4 is the most abstract style of functioning and is characterized by multiple alternative ways of relating to the world based on autonomous internal standards and self-direction. System 4 functioning is oriented toward creative information-seeking and problem-solving. This style of functioning may be illustrated by the phrase, "I'll get all the information and then I'll decide." System 4 persons may be optimally able to see the need for emotional intimacy and to address themselves effectively to evolving it. This person, comprising only 5-7 percent of the population, is inner-directed and uses internally based criteria for guiding his behavior. Gandhi, Einstein, Michelangelo, and Thomas Jefferson could be cited as examples. Although System 4 and System 2 persons are both critical, System 4 persons have alternative proposals and work for their implementation. They are not cynical.

It is obvious that a person's response to the concept of emotional intimacy will depend on the system they operate under. System 1 persons may say, "The whole concept of this book is *Unamerican*!" A System 2 person might observe, "Here is a chance to hurl criticism at the system!" A System 3 person could feel, "Of *course* we need each other!" And a System 4 person may say, "I'll think this over and decide for myself!"

The System 2 person, who will not talk about himself and is most isolated psychologically, is most likely to engage in aggression. This seems to support the theory that a lack of emotional intimacy can indeed be dangerous—for the individual, his immediate society, and mankind.

The presence of intimacy helps human beings to deal with stressful situations. During World War II, the ratio of German camp guards to American prisoners was 1 to 1. However, there were many successful escapes, and morale, in light of the circumstances, was high. Prisoners were held in large group enclosures in those camps. In Korea and Viet Nam, the ratio of prison guards to American prisoners was 1 to 30; yet there were almost no escapes, and morale was abysmally low. In the Asian setting, prisoners were isolated from one another; they gave up, lost hope, and became psychologically disoriented. The intimacy among prisoners in the German camps may have contributed to their survival.

It is possible that similar influences result in similar effects in the present American social order. Perhaps certain citizens lose interest and commitment because the lack of human ties makes it difficult for them to bridge the gap and join the human community.

There is a sort of emotional Hansen's disease (leprosy). In leprosy the disease progresses until small nerve endings are no longer functional. Tactile contact points in arms and legs are then literally worn away without pain due to the nonfunctional nerve endings. Similarly, in emotional leprosy, a person gradually becomes insensitive to his world. Bit by bit, his "contacts" wear away and he is diminished in stature as a fully functioning human being. As physicians point out, the capacity to respond to stimuli by feeling pain is necessary for survival. Without this mechanism, humans and animals would frequently place themselves in danger. Psychologists, making an analogy, say that the capacity for emotion—from distress to joy—is vital to psychological survival. Without the ability to experience emotion, a person has no way to position himself in psychological time and space as he attempts to cope with his changing world. His survival is in jeopardy. Survival is a matter of intimacy!

The recent interest in sensitivity group processes that has touched most educational, religious, business, and psychological settings could also be viewed as an expression of the need to break down inauthentic ways of relating and to establish capacities for intimacy.

The rock music festival phenomenon, such as Woodstock, also may be seen as the expression of a deep wish to be part of a tribe, however transient.

So-called "hippie" or "freaky" attire with its emphasis on elaborate costumes, beautiful hair, and colorful adornments can be seen as an expression of a tribal wish—a wish for a feeling of identity. This need seems more nondirectional than the need for identity expressed by Hitler's Junge, for many members of the youth culture are experiencing the *now* freely, rather than embracing a "heavy mind trip" or a serious job. Many such persons are not actively combating anything, but are simply attempting to live lives in tune with their personal principles. There is often an absence of the "True Believer" mentality and, instead, an expressed wish to be left alone to "do our thing." Residents of the Taos, New Mexico, communes (Reality, New Buffalo, and Morningstar) express these feelings. No one could contend, however, that all residents of these alternate living experiments fit this description.

The interest in communal living in a variety of arrangements, which will be discussed at greater length later, could also be viewed as an expression of the deeply held desire to re-evolve the primary ties that the American family is, sometimes unsuccessfully, attempting to maintain.

As Charles Reich pointed out in *Greening of America*, the people who have become most disenchanted with the American Dream, those whom he describes as belonging to Consciousness 3, are evolving a way of life based on "being" and on dealing with life interdependently on one's own terms. They value human relationships above all else and avoid intellectualizing "verbal gamesmanship" with its associated isolation and alienation.

In important ways people who favor communal life styles have defied the Puritan catechism of "oughts" and "shoulds." They have opted for living arrangements that allow them latitude of action, free from the thundering chorus of societally endorsed rules. To some of them, the traditional family structure seems buried under rules. For the married male: (1) Be faithful; (2) Work as hard as possible to be a good provider; (3) Be strong; (4) Be care-free and playful; (5) Be omnipotent; (6) Be omniscient; and (7) Be potent. For the wife: (1) Serve your husband and children first, yourself second; (2) Be content; (3) Keep a clean house; (4) Attend P.T.A. meetings; (5) Don't compete on any level with your husband; (6) Be sexually satisfying; (7) Be sexually satisfied; (8) Be beautiful in the Hollywood tradition; and (9) *Never* complain.

It should not be surprising that some young people prefer not to labor under the burden of such expectations. In voluntary communal living it is possible for two or more people to evolve their own guidelines and to relearn the capacity to say, "I want!" responsibly, in the context of the emotional intimacy.

2

intimacy hierarchy

Intimacy may be one of the most overworked words in our vocabulary. It is used to sell perfume and all manner of artificial self-enhancement materials. It is used to sell magazines, perfume, and automobiles and to purvey the philosophy of the effective social swinger. It strikes fear in the hearts of many who equate it with sexual irresponsibility and promiscuity.

It may be helpful to conceive of intimacy as a hierarchy of various levels, rather than an either-or proposition. Intimacy can be viewed as a pyramid with three interrelated levels: intellectual, physical, and emotional. In this view all levels are of equal importance, although some seem to be more frequently embraced than others. None should be emphasized to the exclusion of the others, and none should be omitted. It is possible that at birth humans have the potential to fully embrace all levels of intimacy, but in the course of development, many lose their original capacity.

FIGURE II

INTIMACY HIERARCHY

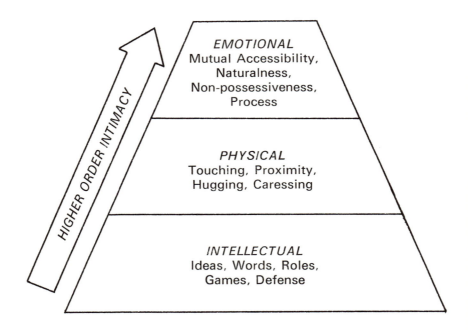

intellectual intimacy

*Though I speak with the tongues of men
and of angels, and have not charity, I
am become as sounding brass, or a tink-
ling cymbal.*

I CORINTHIANS 13:1

How often we've heard that. How *little* we have believed it! Intellectual intimacy is the intimacy of brass and cymbals. It is the intimacy of ideas and verbal interactions. It is the intimacy of the cocktail party, the selling of the social self, and the strictly intellectual classroom experience. People exchange ideas in ways that tend to protect rather than expose their inner selves. Isolation remains. Everyone stays safe in their emotional aloneness. At parties, we strive to be "cool," to appear unruffled, attractive, and invulnerable (except on our own terms).

FACULTY CLUB

What padded cell is this? Island, alone.
Owls in the wood sleep, while a puffy jay
Powders my verbs to isochronic sand,
A bloodless vivisection, song, where imbecile
Is action, filled with pride. The crude world skirts
The island, glides around the castaways.

Emeritus Professor waves the rope
He calls his necktie—S O S—brews leaves
While fledglings pick, echoing him. "Run,
Dash, hoot, match your music with the owls',"
The old man mumbles. "Look at me.
The snowy nightbirds pace my ivory sled."

The ships sail past us, canvas billowing.
Their rigging crawls, arboreal with apes
In action shaping destiny.
The tea like hemlock trembles in my hand.
What island cell is this? Mock jays and owls—
Alas, the necktie! Socrates! What bliss!

—Robert Huff
from Colonel Johnson's Ride

Eric Berne, in *Games People Play*, showed how such games help us *avoid* intimacy, not achieve it. *Who's Afraid of Virginia Woolf*, and *Waiting for Godot* also speak to this point. When games are played to the exclusion of honest interaction the cost is enormous. The script is familiar.

"How are you?"

"I am fine."

"How's work?"

"Fine."

"I like you, and have been thinking about you all evening."

"Let's go somewhere where we can be alone."

"My wife doesn't understand me . . ."

Then, *later*, "I'll call you some-time."

"Goodnight."

In Camus' novel, *The Stranger*, the main character, Meursault, refused to play games, to exchange false social verbiage, and to feign affection that did not exist. His various experiences illustrated well how his isolation seemed to be encouraged by his contemporaries through their superficial, script-playing interchanges. Meursault's attempts to simply be himself resulted in his conviction for murder. For example, when he refused to say he was upset over his mother's death and his killing of an Arab in self-defense, he was branded a "not me" by his society.

The John Wayne syndrome that encourages young men to be ruggedly independent and to need no one is one example of intellectual intimacy. The hero of the movie western or detective story who seems to need no one in order to survive is a high prophet of this form of intimacy. The intimacy at this level is mostly verbal and capacities for it are acquired early in the socialization process. This intimacy is extremely role-oriented and one is more concerned with the self one is conveying than with the self one is.

The plethora of books describing how to be popular, how to win friends and influence people, and how to get ahead in the business world all seem to focus on this superficial intellectual intimacy level.

When I was a child, I spake as a child, I understood as a child, I thought as a child; but when I became a man, I put away childish things.

I CORINTHIANS 13:11

This well-known verse is an accurate description of the "fall" from childlike openness and trust to a "mature" style of relating that is characterized by intellectual and defensive behavior.

It may be useful to adopt the premise that at birth the human being is maximally able to experience intimacy at all levels—emotional, physical, and intellectual. As human development progresses, a person may lose the capacity to experience higher levels of intimacy. As soon as the infant is able to manipulate verbal symbols he begins to acquire from others his "looking-glass self," which he will cling to with great tenacity. He literally learns what he is, what he is not, and what he should be from the responses elicited from others in interactions with them. He is especially rewarded for success at intellectual intimacy, for saying and doing socially acceptable things. In short order, his self is shaped by others in ways consistent with society's conception of "right."

The real goal of survival education may be to free persons from past learning in order to acquire survival skills. Educational institutions may need to get about the business of facilitating *unlearning.* It is assumed here that anyone with enough skill in dealing with verbal symbols to read these printed words is in *need* of help. He is already *maimed* in terms of full human survival. However, much of what currently goes on in organized education is exclusively at the intellectual level of intimacy. The lecture, note-taking, test-taking, competition paradigm best illustrates intellectual intimacy. Students are allowed to become intellectually intimate with an instructor's ideas, but many educators either feel obligated to stifle any higher order intimacy or are unable to participate in high levels of interaction.

Jerry Farber, in his little book *The Student As Nigger*, pointed out that the student's role is similar to that of an indentured servant. They have little influence and are subjected to the control of teachers and administrators. Their second-class status is overseen by administrators on behalf of the whole society. Intellectual, often destructive, intimacy interactions are their lot. As long as they remain deferential and passive they are accepted. But if they should disagree or ask those frightening questions that begin with "Why?" they are termed unruly, unappreciative, disobedient, difficult, and delinquent. They are seldom treated as full persons—as colleagues in the survival task of all men.

PROFESSOR EMERITUS

Old Histrionics, huddled in his chair,
Sophrosýne. He thinks: Hawks hang in air.
Being alone, they do not care
Whether they make man signs aloft
Or just glide there.
Old scholars are but peregrines among
The spoils they have on thorn trees hung
In stiff exhibits from which glass eyes stare.
And I, who emphasized my words
With movements like the motion under birds,

Settle to age without a sign of wings.
What if my students find that springs
In truth lead to meanderings,
If, in tidewater, seeing how things go,
One of them sings?
Passionate minds are full of strife,
And, striving, they can soar right out of life

Or cling to such inconsequential things
As making magic in young ears.
Mimic impassioned voices forty years

And teaching is a kind of poetry,
A way of shaping knowledge on the lee
Side of the world effectively.
I used to dream of shanghaiing
All young minds for the sea
By rolling at them riddles of the kind
Which have no answers, save the ones we find
In travelogues big as the Odyssey,
When I was apt at illustrating tales
With movements like the motion of great whales.

—Robert Huff
from Colonel Johnson's Ride

The educational system in this country still shows the influence of the Puritans and the clergymen who became the administrators of the early New England colleges. College and university administrators, representing society's conservative ruling elite, worry endlessly about how to control student behavior in dormitories. They have been appointed *in loco parentis*—the parent's representatives—so sexual activities, drinking, and housekeeping are of great concern to them. This is amazing when one realizes that the student's age mates who went directly into the world of work after high school are accepted as responsible. No one polices the halls or living quarters of the urban apartment houses. Our society guarantees the rights of working youth. It does *not* guarantee similar rights to the student-nigger.

In L. Frank Baum's delightful story, *The Wonderful Wizard of Oz*, written in the year 1900, several characters illustrate how persons learn and believe in unfounded assumptions about their personal limitations. Dorothy and her dog Toto want to return to Kansas, the Scarecrow wants a brain, the Tin Woodman wants a heart, and the Cowardly Lion wants courage.

The Scarecrow learned he had no brain. An old crow said to him, "If you only had brains in your head you would be as good a man as any of them. Brains are the only things worth having in this world, no matter whether one is a crow or a man."

The Tin Woodman loved a Munchkin girl and was prevented from marrying her by the Wicked Witch of the East. She caused a series of accidents followed by a succession of replacement operations by a tin-smith until the woodman was *all* tin. He was convinced that without a "heart" he couldn't care for anyone.

The Cowardly Lion was convinced that he lacked the courage shown by other lions. He was constantly afraid of everything.

All the characters felt that only the Great Wizard of Oz could solve their problems. They were most distressed when the never-seen wizard was exposed as an impotent charlatan. He said, "I'm just a common man!" In response to their continued insistence he finally gave the Scarecrow a head full of bran and sawdust for a brain, the Tin Woodman a velvet-sawdust heart, and the Cowardly Lion a courage potion to drink. Other versions of the story have him giving the Scarecrow a diploma, the Tin Woodman a small clock "heart" and the Cowardly Lion a medal. The point remains.

When the story is examined it can be seen that throughout the adventures of the characters the Scarecrow was the problem-solver, the Tin Woodman was continually weeping over the plight of a crushed beetle and other misfortunes and was beginning to rust, and the Cowardly Lion was consistently courageous. In short, each possessed those capacities he had been taught, either by others or by experience, that he lacked.

The similarity between Dorothy's friends and many real people is worth noting. We all know people who feel obliged to earn certificates and diplomas (bestowed by wizards) to have proof of their intellectual prowess. Psychologically maimed persons seek out various wizards whom they have enthroned as omnipotent and omniscient. Psychotherapists, professors, teachers, parents, advice-giving columnists, spouses, and friends are all commonly chosen as wizards. When they are revealed sooner or later as "common men," the searcher is disappointed and angry. We need to begin realizing our capacities already exist and no magician is needed to help us unlearn the internally accepted limits, which we have been carefully taught.

It is amusing to think about the need for unlearning and relearning following our mastery of the intellectual intimacy level in order that we may redevelop capacities for productive physical and emotional intimacy. It could be proposed that a certain block of courses be experienced by students at all levels in educational structures. Teachers-in-training, who will exert such a profound influence on children, should certainly be exposed. The following block of courses may serve to illustrate the point:

> De-educational Psychology
> Philosophy and History of De-education
> Need for De-education
> De-education for What is Real
> Practicum in De-education
> Theories in De-education
> Techniques of De-education
> The De-educator's Role
> Organization and Administration of De-education
> Individual Similarities
> The De-educated Personality (Healthy Personality)
> Personality Dynamics and De-education

Although we like to think that speech is one of the important ways in which people set up in-depth communication processes, it is possible that speech is most often used to keep others *away* by relating in terms of roles. Speech may be one of the most popular distance tools!

Spoken English (in the U.S.) has some very interesting characteristics. Our language has many words, with various connotations and denotations, to describe hostility. The words seem to form a continuum:

> I am distressed, troubled, irritated, perturbed,
> uncomfortable, disgusted, incensed, angry, hostile.

The highest level of hostility is expressed by "I want to *kill* you," or "I *hate* you." The English language, as it is commonly used, however, offers very few words for describing emotional intimacy. Love, tenderness, gentleness, and caring seem to exhaust the available terms.

English, as it is currently spoken in this country, is a pauper's language. The Greeks used ten words to refer to the various qualities of love ranging from agape to eros; modern English uses one word only—love.

Abraham Maslow, the noted humanistic psychologist who was deeply concerned with the barriers to full human functioning, studied the healthy, self-actualized person, and concluded that the English language was "rotten for good people." He maintained that the vocabulary for the virtues was terribly limited. He was fond of pointing out that even our word *love* was "all smeared up" with various connotations and denotations. Our country's preoccupation with hostility and dissonance seems revealed in the number of terms we have evolved to describe such acitvities. Both naivete and inexperience with emotional intimacy are revealed by the *lack* of terms used communicating in this area. In fact, we seem to delight in the search for negativity. This will be discussed further in the "Gospel According to Chicken Little" (Part II).

physical intimacy

In discussing physical intimacy, we will examine the dilemma of the emerging adolescent behavior, women's liberation, prostitution, pornography, sex education, and the ideas of Desmond Morris as expressed in his new book *Intimate Behaviour.* Physical intimacy is a "loaded" area. The very term draws strong reactions from most people. How can one remain disinterested in the one area of life perhaps most laden with taboos, "oughts" and "shoulds," and guilt feelings?

KNOW ME

Come this way
to know me:
Lie gently in
my arms.   *I'd rather talk.*

Move closer
and feel my lips
with the touch
of you.   *I'd rather talk.*

Let me feel
what covers your heart
and hides your softness
from me.   *I must talk.*

Let me move
my hand
onto your complete
warm softness.   *I don't love you.*

You thought I
loved you?   *Yes.*

Take this way
to know me:
Lie gently in
my arms.

—Don Decker

For most people in our culture,
physical intimacy is more frightening than intellectual inti-

macy because physical intimacy is marketed as the highest order. Popular magazines, advertising, literature, and films all portray physical intimacy as the god at whose altar all should worship.

Initial experiences with physical intimacy are often disappointing, especially when all hopes for escape from a state of isolation are based on such experiences. The taboo against teachers touching children in the classroom illustrates that the fear of physical intimacy is inextricably bound to an equally intense need for it in educational processes.

SCORPIO IN WINTER WAITING FOR SUMMER

(on being told by a Sister Scorpio that July would be a positive turning point for us)

Hellbent as Baudelaire,
I feel the year shift its gears,
grinding out of autumn
into winter.

Hope is an iceberg
rising like a steeple dead center
in a universal waste.
I wait

for something
to happen, dug in like a claw
on the iceberg's point:
the cough

of an engine
winning its way of life again,
the season speed—
shifting

into spring.
But all I hear is the hiss
of steam—the sun

And Hell
frozen over still is Hell.
And yet—and yet
I am

a Scorpio.
So I can wait for a judicial
July, like Saratoga
the turning

point in a
bad war, when engines will
purr like kittens,
when every-

thing will
shift smoothly into third gear,
and Hell will be
hot once more.

—*George Drew*

The American formula for growing up is tied to our worship at the altar of physical intimacy. Adolescents often complain of the isolation and sterility of their lives. Holden Caulfield, the main character in J. D. Salinger's *Catcher in the Rye* set out on a personal odyssey to discover routes to connectedness. The poignant story shows the lack of meaningful human ties in his life and his faltering attempts to find himself. The Beatles recorded a song describing a young girl who quietly leaves home "after living alone for so many years."

GOING OUT

The day she left
The bay water turned turbulent
And clouds congregated over the surface
Like squadrons of clipper ships
With sails fully unfurled;
And as the wind
Whispered the cumulus fleet across the bay
And out to sea,
She pointed toward the shore and said:
"Oh look, the tide is going out!"
But she herself
Surged against the driftwood land,
A knuckled wave knocking the coast
Of our distress.

—George Drew

Very often parents respond to the child's expression of loneliness by sawing that adolescence is a time for learning and achievement and one day their child will be going about his or her daily routine and all at once Prince or Princess Charming will appear. The world will stop, the sun will rotate, and talcum powder will fall from the trees. (If it *is* prince charming, *hopefully* he will be a graduate of an excellent medical school and be of similar ethnic and racial origin.) The American myth continues by demanding an appropriate period of engagement—perhaps six months—and after waiting patiently, the youngster will be rewarded on the wedding night by discovering how close two persons can be. Not all play this drama according to the script! After the junior-senior prom and a little imbibing, some fall from "grace" by experimenting with physical intimacy in the back seat of a station wagon. Whether experienced by the honeymoon couple at the New Beginnings Motel or by the renegades in the station wagon, sexual physical intimacy is often very tremendously disillusioning. Some have discovered that physical intimacy is not the highest form of intimacy and does not guarantee full human sharing. Nevertheless, the myth is still embraced by the majority of young people.

The plight of women in the American way of life has been discussed by the feminist leader Germaine Greer, whose bestselling book *The Female Eunuch* appeared in America in 1971. She feels that women have been relegated to second class citizenship. Their plight is even more unfortunate than the racial minorities because women have, as yet, no sense of unity. Because physical intimacy is a status symbol for a man, women are used for physical pleasure much as a master uses his slave. Greer feels that until both women and men discard the "I'll use you" attitude, no real human emotional intimacy can be evolved. She deplores the *Playboy* philosophy, its pictures of immature girls, and its emphasis on physical intimacy. She goes beyond the hackneyed militaristic style of some of her colleagues in the feminist movement in that she feels it is pointless to blame either sex for the dehumanizing rules controlling human relationships. She prefers to point the finger at historical, political, economic, and psychological factors. She is also very critical of the nuclear family structure in which the mother can be, and often is, controlled by the child. Although she has never lived in a commune, she feels that communal arrangements in some form, will play an important role in the future.

In our culture physical intimacy is very often conditional. The bride-to-be says, "You may touch me only after we are married." The segregationist says, "You can come close to me if you are of my race."

Our society sets very definite limits on physical intimacy. For example, no one hesitates to allow a physician to touch them, yet if a man on the street were to take the same liberties he would be arrested for assault. Our society very carefully certificates those persons allowed to deal in intimacy. Physicians, psychiatrists, psychologists, dentists, and beauticians are examples.

One of the major areas of social concern with physical intimacy is that of prostitution. This enterprise could be viewed as a nonsocially sanctioned form of physical intimacy and may be meeting a need that is caused by the social system as it is currently structured. Germaine Greer might define the role of wives in some marriages as a sanctioned form of prostitution!

Pornography may be a substitute form of physical intimacy. Although we can't even define what it is, many people persist in feeling it is evil. Despite increasing amounts of evidence to the contrary, they are convinced that exposure to pornographic materials will warp young minds.

In *Intimacy, Sensitivity, Sex, and the Art of Love* Allen and Martin reported that in Denmark, where pornography has recently been legalized, there has been a marked and continuing diminution of sexual crime. Researchers in America have found that rapists and child molesters actually received *less* exposure to pornographic materials during adolescence than normal heterosexual adults. One study conducted by Dr. Michael J. Goldstein of the University of California at Los Angeles and Harold S. Kant, Director of California's Legal and Behavioral Institute, compared 60 men convicted of or charged with sex offenses, with 52 regular patrons of pornography shops, and 63 "solid citizens" as a "control." The results revealed that all the sexual deviates shared one common characteristic; they had *little* exposure to erotica when they were adolescents. The normal adults in the sample reported more experience with pornography both as teenagers and adults than did the sex offenders. There was no evidence to support a connection between sex crimes and pornography. The researchers concluded that "a reasonable exposure to erotica, particularly during adolescence, reflects a high degree of sexual interest and curiosity that correlates with adult patterns of acceptable heterosexual interest and practice."

According to Allen and Martin, the recent *Report of the Commission on Pornography and Obscenity* compiled by a group of social scientists at the request of the President suggested that our laws governing obscenity were obsolete and that we should follow the Danes' example and make pornography legal, at least for adults. Our collective inability to deal with these matters seems revealed in that the report, which cost two million dollars, has been ignored; perhaps it just doesn't happen to agree with our traditional "oughts" and "shoulds."

Similarly, the recent *Report of the National Commission on Marijuana and Drug Abuse* recommending the abolishment of criminal penalties for the private use of marijuana may be ignored. When traditional rules are challenged many prefer not to examine the old ways, but to ignore the criticism. The Lily Pad Theory in Part II will explore this.

Perhaps our traditional "oughts" and "shoulds" concerning physical intimacy encourage us to do violence to our youth in a variety of other areas such as sex education, or perhaps one should say the lack of it. Such programs are intensely controversial and students often receive a watered-down mixture of anatomical and physiological "facts." Almost no attention is paid to the evolvement of full human intimacy.

The most recent additions in the American tradition of how-to-do-it manuals includes *The Sensuous Woman, The Sensuous Man, The Sensuous Couple,* and *The Sensuous Child!* These books take a plumbing approach to physical intimacy. *The Sensuous Child*, supposedly written by a 13-year-old, tells how to be successful in spying on bathroom activities; the *Sensuous Couple* gives guidelines for undressing! What next? Perhaps the *Sensuous Senior Citizen* and the *Sensuous Neonate!* That should exhaust the age range. Although some of these books were allegedly written as spoofs of the American view of intimacy, it seems that many readers have taken them seriously and feel more liberated for having read them.

Feminists like Germaine Greer would hold up such manuals as evidence of our misguided approach to a misunderstood goal. How can we find the way to intimacy if we have erroneous ideas about it? Such books may actually discourage the development of relationships that contain elements of real human intimacy. Instead, they encourage sexual athletic competition in the highest tradition of intellectual intimacy.

Rules and regulations regarding physical behavior vary from culture to culture. Diplomats going to South American posts are not accustomed to the Latin habit of standing very close to someone even for routine conversation. American servicemen are amazed to see men friends commonly holding hands in certain Asian cultures.

Within the American social system, women are free to hug and carress more intensely and over longer periods of time than are men. Two men holding hands would attract attention while two women would not.

The fear of intimacy in marriage can be best illustrated by the fable of the freezing porcupines. The two animals were huddled together for warmth, but were repelled by the sting of each other's quills. Each time the need for warmth brought them together, their mutual irirtation began anew. The porcupines were continually being driven together and forced apart because of their need for intimacy. One would be hard-pressed to find a better description of the neurotic interaction in some marriages. Deeply felt needs for intimacy draw partners together while the interaction of carefully taught inhibitions drives them apart.

In his most recent book, *Intimate Behaviour*, the famous zoologist Desmond Morris described his observations of physical intimacy processes among humans. His comments extend the work on infant monkeys done by Harry Harlow into the human context. Morris feels that intimacy in a full sense cannot occur *without* bodily contact and that such intimacy is a matter of survival. This was certainly the case with Harlow's infant monkeys who, when deprived of bodily contact with mothers and peers, often showed mental and physical impairment in later years.

According to Morris, human intimate contact can range from the first glance to casual touching to the mating act. He divided the usual human sequence of contact between men and women into twelve stages; (1) eye to body, (2) eye to eye, (3) voice to voice, (4) hand to hand, (5) arm to shoulder, (6) arm to waist, (7) mouth to mouth, (8) hand to head, (9) hand to body, (10) mouth to breast, (11) hand to genitals, and (12) genitals to genitals. Progression through these stages, in some fashion or other, is seen as a useful screening device en route to an intimate "bonding." The sex act itself strongly influences depth bonding, except, of course, in the case of rape, which is characterized by an omission of the intermediate stages in the usual human contact sequence. The matter of human bonding is a serious business, for once the bond is established, emotional disengagement from the bond may be difficult.

People who have experienced an unfortunate bonding may be haunted by regret or may be unable to stop caring. They may say, "I'm still thinking of him (her) all the time!"

According to Morris, when true bond-mates are unavailable, humans turn to a variety of culturally accepted substitute sources for physical intimacy. Doctor's offices, beauty parlors, barber shops, cigarettes, pets, and even one's own body are used. Clutching oneself in times of stress illustrates this last substitute.

LET'S BE PEOPLE

For a few minutes
Can we be people
Instead of positions?
Can I be I
And you be you
And free?
Can you judge me
And I judge you
As a person
And not as a position?
Can you react to me
And I react to you,
Without thinking
Of what you should be doing,
Because of your position,
And what I should be doing,
Because of my position?
Can people just be people
Together, and for once, escape
The boundaries of assumed correctness
Imposed by those who assume
They must react to a position
Instead of a person?

Why do people attach more importance
To position than to people?
Silly, isn't it?
Why do people attach more importance
To their positions
Than to themselves?
Sillier, isn't it?

—*Don Decker*

Physical intimacy is a matter of survival and full human intimacy includes it as an important component along with the intellectual and emotional levels.

emotional intimacy

The highest level of intimacy is viewed here as emotional intimacy. Emotional intimacy is the level for which we are least equipped in terms of past experiences. Emotional intimacy has four characteristics that are important to this discussion: mutual accessibility, naturalness, nonpossessiveness, and process.

MUTUAL ACCESSIBILITY

Persons enjoying an emotionally intimate relationships, as a couple or as a group, tend to see each other as *mutually accessible.* Each person feels he has complete access to the other—free of criticism. The emphasis here is upon *mutual* accessibility. Traditional psychotherapy is not mutual; it could be viewed as one-way accessibility in which the client pays the therapist to enter the client's world. The client is accessible. The therapist and his inner world are not.

Accessibility in emotional intimacy could also be viewed as a continuum including "no way" accessibility, "one way" accessibility, and "mutual" accessibility. Different schools of thought on human behavior could be ranked along this continuum. Recent developments in the science of behavior modification based on stimulus-response psychology contend that no accessibility, in terms of the internal worlds of therapist and client, is required in order for positive gains to be made. Through a system of reward and punishment, the client can change or eliminate undesirable behavior. Many psychoanalytically oriented therapists, drawing upon the classic Freudian model, advance the merits of a one-way communication system wherein the therapist remains a closed system to the client. The most strict advocates of this theory place the therapist outside of the client's fiield of vision during the sessions. Many perceptual, humanistically oriented psychologists believe deeply in the mutually accessible relationship. Although they certainly do not feel that a therapist should unburden himself to a client, they do hold that the therapist should reveal himself to those he helps. If the therapist is tired or angry, he feels it is his responsibility not to hide his feelings.

Accessibility must be seen in terms of a specific relationship, but it has universal implications. The healthy self-actualized person is comfortable in both offering and taking advantage of accessibility. Experienced therapists of various schools of thought often report that as a client learns to function fully he tends to see the therapist as a colleague rather than an all-knowing wizard. The therapist is gradually "demoted" from wizard status to colleague. The relationship begins to show more mutual accessibility, naturalness, less role orientation, and more process orientation.

DURING THE LAST SNOW

I lay in bed
watching flakes
flow by the glass
like big albino
butterflies. The
world was covered

with butterflies!
In the dark room
my woman's white
butterfly beauty
waxed uncertainly;
but as the dark
began to vanish,
the butterfly flakes
flew away into
the sky's cocoon,
my woman awoke,
and we toboganned on
the sleds of our skin
toward the dawn.

—George Drew

Persons who advertise an accessibility they will not or cannot deliver may exert a negative influence on prospective aid-seekers. Instructors, therapists, and others may indicate, verbally or otherwise, "I am available to you whenever you need me." Yet, in fact, they are often not available. This hypocrisy may cause cynicism on the part of prospective helpees. Instructors who claim availability, but who haven't enough time and energy for all students are often guilty of this cue versus practice gap. They lose credibility and are discounted by students to the extent that such a gap is discovered.

Authenticity and honesty can prevent a breakdown in credibility. In short, an honest non-available person may exert a much more positive influence than a person claiming a nonexistent availability. The latter is soon found out.

Ideally, an instructor should be available at all times to all students. But limited time and energy prohibit such a broad range of availability for many faculty members. Honest exposure of such limits seems the only educationally sound approach to this dilemma.

The concept of accessibility in human relationships is critical in view of the developing construct of emotional intimacy. What are the necessary and sufficient conditions that enable one person to view another person as intellectually, physically, and emotionally accessible?

In a recent study that the author carried out at a large midwestern university, student preferences for sources of help were studied. Thirty hypothetical crisis situations were presented to 633 students; they were asked where they would turn for help with the problems. Nearly 19,000 responses were examined. Helping professionals in university counseling centers and on residence hall staffs claim that they are perceived as accessible. The student responses showed otherwise. Seventy percent of all student problems would be taken to other students, faculty members, or others *rather* than to professional helpers. In fact, as many students chose peers *only* as chose professional personnel. This is especially significant since the crises were severe. Some of the 30 hypothetical crisis situations were: "I think I am pregnant." "I think a girl is pregnant because of me." "I'm so depressed and tired—I don't really care what happens anymore!"

The accessibility of the helper must be perceived by needful persons, or, in a real sense, it doesn't exist. The results of this university study also support the development of the peer-helper concept. In this type of program students who have been given some orientation to the task and their limitations are involved in helping their peers. Careful planning can result in a highly effective and nonthreatening referral system for serious difficulties.

HELPER (person wanting to help another)

The establishment of the helping relationship seems to be facilitated by a continuum of cues which the helper furnishes to enable the helpee to see him as accessible. The cues are both verbal and nonverbal.

Verbalization is probably the most often used and least demanding method. Cues that are ranked above this purely intellectual form may involve more activity on the part of the helper—leaving his office door open, receiving clients warmly, and even pursuing ambivalent clients. Such verbal and nonverbal conditions of accessibility, as furnished by a helper, could be measured on a behavioral dimension. Research studies could then explore the conditions of availability furnished, the style of their provision, and their influence on needful persons.

The effective helper seems capable of offering intellectual, physical, and emotional intimacy to people who seek him out for help. He especially furnishes the conditions of emotional intimacy. Such a helper encourages accessibility, naturalness, and nonpossessiveness and he acts on his commitment to the therapeutic process by directing his expertise toward its evolvement. The conditions of accessibility discussed here in terms of the helper-helpee relationship apply equally to all human relationships at all social levels.

HELPEE (person wanting help from another)

Certain conditions must exist within the helpee if he is to perceive another as accessible. He must feel a push to reach out and must perceive the possible helper as palatable, nonthreatening, and in possession of some survival benefits. No matter how effective the helper could be once the relationship is established, if he is not perceived as accessible there will be no relationship.

At various times in our relationships, we all adopt either the helper or helpee roles. One purpose of this book is to furnish a psychological rationale for our reaching out when we need human warmth and for our furnishing accessibility to those who need us. We must realize such accessibility is a matter of psychological survival.

The abrupt loss of an emotionally intimate accessible relationship can cause severe difficulty for all of us. The loss of a life partner is commonly followed by a period of listlessness, grief, apathy, and depression. It is only after a lengthy period in which attempts are made to establish new relationships that such persons regain a feeling of stability and report a renewed feeling about the meaning in life.

Even though a marriage may have lacked positive features, the emotionally tumultuous time following a divorce can literally incapacitate men and women. The passage of time is seldom enough to help someone regain their emotional footing. It is only when new relationships—either romantic or platonic—are established that persons resume their momentum in coping with life.

In our culture, aging is often accompanied by increased alienation from the mainstream of society. Many people see aging as alien to the self and tend to repress their feelings of distaste and anxiety. Old people are looked upon as "not me" because it is too unpleasant to think of oneself as aged. There is very little accessibility between the young and the old.

Retirement communities should provide the aged with the opportunity to establish new relationships and evolve new ways of coping with the problems of aging. Unfortunately, all too often, a highly structured regimen is imposed on senior citizens. After a lifetime of being told what to do—in childhood, in elementary, secondary, and college environments, and on the job for 30 years—the hoary-headed residents are often subjected to more rules and planned activities. It is sad to see the aged conform to schedules—breakfast at 8:00, shuffleboard at 9:30, lunch at 1:00—or obediently answering the cry of the recreational therapist, *"It's volley ball time!"*

The recent movie *Kotch* reveals the basic human revulsion with the programmed community death programs. *Kotch* shows middle class values and morality as confused and the mature man who is sensitive to this prejudice and misunderstanding. He is completely aware of the limited value in retirement corrals and he is not ready to surrender to family pressures. Instead, he takes a Greyhound trip and delivers a baby in a service station restroom.

NATURALNESS

The emotionally intimate relationship is *natural* in the sense that the Greek Stoics used the word. Persons are accepted as they are, not for their ability to change themselves to meet another's requirements or to play a role assigned to them by others. The conditions for facilitating human interaction (genuineness, unconditional positive regard, warmth, and acceptance) as defined by Carl Rogers, Charles Truax, and Robert Carkhuff are included in this concept of a natural, role-free interaction. People are free to be themselves, to expose their frailities and strengths. Hopefully, they are mutually empathetic in that they can see the world as the other person sees it. Lastly, there should be nonconditional acceptance of the other's natural way of being in the world. Persons are accepted although their behavior may not always be condoned.

The emotionally intimate relationship is an interaction between *human beings*, not *roles*. It is a case of person "A" relating to person "B," not a teacher relating to a student, a therapist to a client, or a superior individual to an inferior one. The emphasis is upon human similarities not human differences.

To set out to attain emotional intimacy as an "assignment" may be self-defeating. If we desire the relationship too highly, we may attempt to change ourselves and become unnatural in order to meet our idea of what the other person will approve. By changing ourselves we have destroyed all chance for a person-to-person relationship, for we are now playing a *role.*

The expressions of young people—"let it be," "don't be other directed"—are indications of their desire for natural relationships. We all want to have feelings of self-worth that are not wholly derived from others. Frederick Perls, the founder of Gestalt therapy, has expressed these sentiments in a poetic statement which is now used on the posters so popular with students:

> *I do my thing, and you do your thing.*
> *I am not in this world to live up to your expectations*
> *and you are not in this world to live up to mine.*
> *You are you and I am I,*
> *and if by chance we find each other, it's beautiful.*
> *If not, it can't be helped . . .*
> —*Frederick S. Perls*

In natural relationships, feelings are of ultimate importance and are highly respected. When we choose to or are forced to hide our real selves—our feelings—we begin to "leave" psychologically. Anyone who has attended a meeting and begun to feel angry without feeling free to express the anger has experienced this. We begin to be bored and restless, and we start thinking of other things. Our unexpressed feelings cause us to pull out psychologically, much as a train pulls out of a station. Contrary to our expectations, however, when we do express such feelings in a meeting we often find others share our perceptions, and real communication begins again. When we remain silent we usually think, "If only I would have said something! Next time I will!"

Mainstream society often requires that disadvantaged and disenfranchised groups transform themselves and subdue their feelings as a condition of acceptance into the social order. Relationships with such disenfranchised persons are conditional upon their adoption of a life style palatable to the existing social structure. This requirement may be the cause of our difficulties with minority groups.

The experiences of Meursault, Camus' main character in *The Stranger*, a classic story of alienation, illustrate that being natural in unnatural surroundings can be dangerous. Meursault refused to lie about his feelings concerning the death of his aging mother. He related events unemotionally and refused to inflate his feelings. Immediately, society felt menaced. They asked him, for example, to say that he regretted murdering an Arab in self-defense. He

replied that what he felt about the matter was more akin to
ennui (vexation, annoyance, chagrin, boredom) than to regret.
This nuance condemned him. According to the foreword that
Camus wrote to one English translation of his work, Meursault
was motivated by a passion for the absolute and for truth,
especially in the area of human relationships. In a real sense,
Meursault accepts "dying for the truth." It is interesting that
many readers of *The Stranger* see Meursault as ill, strange, or
monster-like (a creature-feature character?) when Camus'
intent was to portray a *natural* man!

Challenging the "oughts" and
"shoulds" that demand unnatural behavior forms the central
theme of a literary style that is called black humor. In Joseph
Heller's novel *Catch 22*, the main character, Yossarian, lives
by a sane, natural code in an insane world. He questions the
morality of war after watching the slaughter of his friends,
and adopts the logic of survival. He reasons that if he is psychologically ill, he isn't fit for combat. But Catch 22 is in-
voked against him. Catch 22 is the loophole the authorities
can use to revoke one's rights whenever it suits them. Yossarian's superiors reason that since he realizes he is not well,
he must be sane and fit for combat. He was not allowed to be
natural. He was forced to adapt to an insane world.

NONPOSSESSIVENESS

The third characteristic of
emotional intimacy is nonpossessiveness. Intimacy cannot be
based on "I'll love you if you love me too!" Caring, on the
highest level, delights in the independence of others, not in
the possession of them.

A truly emotionally intimate
relationship cannot exist between "superior" and "inferior"
individuals. The treatment of children as little persons who are
smaller in stature but just as sacred as adults meets this
requirement. Treating children as chattel does not.

Parents often find it difficult to
see their children as individuals. Researchers of the "battered
child syndrome" have found that many parents who beat
their children do so because they see in the child certain
aspects of their own personality that they cannot tolerate.

Their actions are a mixture of self-hate and the desire to rid the child of the undesirable attribute. Insecure, rigid parents often batter their children to death, ostensibly for the child's own good!

ELIZABETHAN

Decked out in yellow,
She sallies forth to meet a green spring,
Fully aware of all her womanly worth,
Despite the love affair gone bad
That plagues her like a broken wing,

And, feeling the eyes
Of others on her as she strolls slowly
Along the walk, a mobile masterpiece,
She moves her parts so as to cause
In them a hush that's almost holy,

Arching her eyes
Smartly, which are as green as spring,
And tossing out her auburn hair, which flows
Over her shoulders, brushing them
As lightly as the tip of a wing,

And fingers her wedding
Ring restively as she struts slowly
On, like an Elizabethan sonnet,
Out of the spring and into summer,
A pagan who is somehow holy.

—George Drew

The highest order intimacy, emotional, exists when we are nonpossessive. Many marriages flounder when one party attempts to possess the other. This smothering eventually destroys an intimate relationship which otherwise might have flourished.

When we view life as an unfolding process it is easier to be nonpossessive. To the extent we see our roles as prescribed (father, husband, daughter), we will attempt to possess others in order to fulfill our assigned role.

To share but not to possess is a large order. Even some psychotherapists lose their effectiveness because they are unable to see that they should be freeing, not possessing, their clients in a dependent relationship.

The turmoil in families often associated with the child's struggle for independence and autonomy also illustrates that for most of us the capacity for intimacy of a nonpossessive nature needs to be learned the hard way.

PROCESS

Lastly, the attainment and maintenance of emotional intimacy is a *process* that requires *constant attention*. When time and energy are not expended to maintain this process, entropy sets in and the relationship deteriorates. It seems clear that emotional intimacy as an experience is a higher order capacity for human beings, and includes both intellectual and physical components.

The "state" of emotional intimacy is one that is never attained once and for all. It is evolved, maintained, and enhanced only by constant effort which leads to total consciousness.

Divorce could be viewed as the failure to evolve and/or maintain emotional intimacy. After emotional intimacy disappears, physical intimacy follows, soon only the chatter about daily routine (intellectual intimacy) remains.

Apart from its religious significance, a marriage ceremony could be seen as a simple verbal and nonverbal statement by two persons: "We have agreed to put some extra effort into our attempt at evolving higher order intimacy with each other. We intend to invest time and energy in the process of intimacy over an extended period of time."

One client commented movingly on the breakdown of her marriage; early in a series of sessions she said, "We don't share as openly as we once did. He withholds things from me. He is distant from me." Perhaps this signalled the loss of emotional intimacy. She reported some weeks alter, "He comes home, takes a shower, runs to the bedroom, and shouts, 'Come in here!' Sex is just a duty for me now!" Evidently, only the physical and intellectual levels were still present. One month later she reported, "I have been *relieved* of my duties! We just sit around trying to maintain polite small talk about the yard, car, and our social calendar." Evidently, all that remained at this point was the intellectual level. In this case, since neither spouse valued the relationship highly (did not choose to attend to process) a divorce, perhaps in the best interests of both parties, quickly followed.

We would conclude that if people really embraced the need they have for intimacy almost any two persons could establish and maintain such a relationship. Some of the science-fiction movies that depict the last two survivors of a holocaust may indicate this. If two persons really needed each other for survival, they *would* invest the time and energy required to establish some form of higher order intimacy as a life-support system. Small requirements of personal taste would soon be dropped and the large benefits of the relationship would be paramount.

The following statement by Henry Ford seems to capture the idea that we must "attend" to relationships as a part of effectively working together:

> *Coming together is a beginning; keeping together is progress, working together is success.*
>
> —*Henry Ford*
> *as quoted by S. M. Basta*
> *University of Nevada*

The expenditure of time and energy on the process does *not* mean we must work to change ourselves. The real work is in pushing back the thundering chorus of traditional "oughts" and "shoulds" which advises us *not* to be intellectually, physically, or emotionally intimate. It is a full-time task to break through these "no-nos." Especially at the emotional intimacy level, much of what we have been taught leads us to resist accessibility, naturalness, and non-possessiveness. Lastly, and perhaps most importantly, we fail to realize the process is worth it! The task of freeing ourselves from the "oughts" and "shoulds" which endanger our individual and collective welfare is demanding and never ending. It is also crucial to our survival.

3

summary

We are generally unprepared to evolve, maintain, and enhance emotionally intimate relationships because of our background. The fear of intimacy is the theme of many works of literature concerning the anti-hero. Salinger's *Catcher In The Rye* and Camus' *The Stranger* illustrate this point.

As we become more intimate with each other, we exert a greater influence on each other's internal worlds. One might define the most open, nurtured relationship between two people as the relationship with the highest level of emotional intimacy.

Once established, emotional intimacy can be constructive or destructive.

Figure III indicates that as increased amounts of intimacy are present in a relationship the potential for both positive and negative influence increases. The extreme example of positive influence would be the god figure—a force for good—with whom we are very intimate. The opposite extreme is represented by the devil. Again, inti-

FIGURE III

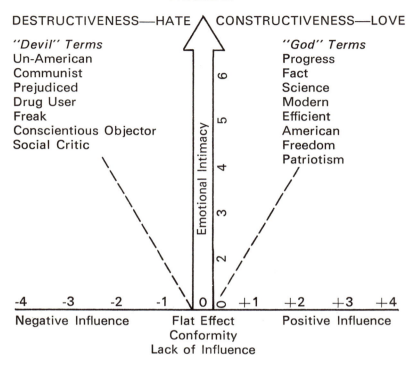

DESTRUCTIVENESS—HATE   CONSTRUCTIVENESS—LOVE

"Devil" Terms
Un-American
Communist
Prejudiced
Drug User
Freak
Conscientious Objector
Social Critic

"God" Terms
Progress
Fact
Science
Modern
Efficient
American
Freedom
Patriotism

Emotional Intimacy

-4   -3   -2   -1   0   +1   +2   +3   +4

Negative Influence   Flat Effect   Positive Influence
                            Conformity
                            Lack of Influence

macy is present but the influence is destructive. We even echo elements of our Puritan heritage and say, "He is possessed by the devil!" when someone is destructive. The popular American comedian Flip Wilson has made that phrase his trademark. He says, "The devil made me do it!"

In his book, *The Ethics of Rhetoric*, Richard Weaver discussed the ways in which people using persuasive techniques apply labels or "ultimate terms" to their opponent's causes in order to create "not me" categories and reduce intimacy. In this country, some of the current god terms are: progress, fact, science, modern, efficient, American, and freedom. Merely identifying a cause with such terms increases the likelihood that voters will favor the cause. Some of the devil terms are: Unamerican, Communist, and prejudiced. Again, merely associating a cause with these terms marshals resistance to the movement. One is reminded of the Joseph McCarthy period in American politics.

Apparently, our god and devil terms—those terms connoting positive and negative forces—are in a constant process of re-alignment. At the close of World War II, the Russians were our allies (god term). Following Sputnik in 1956, the Russians gradually became defined as our enemy (devil term). For a while it appeared we would reach *rapprochement* with the Russians and our "devil" became the Chinese. Following President Nixon's recent visit to China, however, we are changing our view again.

It is difficult to keep up with the terms used to influence us in directions others choose for us. Pacification program means napalm bombing. The Defense Department plans the offensive and the military-business establishment claims to be in the "peace" business!

Many dehumanizing, manipulative processes are founded upon the prior achievement of some degree of emotional intimacy with the victim. It is the contention of this book, however, that, for the most part, as the results of the Milgram studies on obedience illustrated, emotional intimacy tends to decrease the likelihood of negative effects of relationships. It is difficult to hurt a "me!"

The noted anthropologist Ashley Montagu is fond of defining a love relationship as one in which there is a mutual conferring of survival benefits. The position advanced in this book is quite consistent with his definition. An emotionally intimate relationship has the potential to contribute greatly to the "life-support system" of each of us.

Incomplete emotional intimacy is very often conditional. People say, "If you care for me, then I will care for you." The fully functioning, open person is conceptualized here as a person able to function with relatively unconditional intellectual, physical, and emotional intimacy within the limits of responsible behavior. One way to view in-group-out-group distinctions is to say that in-group members relate among themselves at higher intimacy levels than out-group members are able to achieve with members of the group. In an extension of this consideration, current interest in sensitivity groups, and even some elements of the drug culture, can be seen as attempts to achieve high intimacy levels among group members.

The intimacy hierarchy relates to the three consciousness levels discussed by Charles Reich in *Greening of America.* The Consciousness I person concentrates on the physical mastery of his environment through application of his intellectual tools. As a "rugged individual" he manipulates things to tame a wild land. He amasses capital and strives for survival against formidable odds. The corporate Consciousness II man also applies intellectual and physical intimacy capacities as he competes within corporate structures for his feelings of worth and identity. The Consciousness III person seems to be more attuned to emotional intimacy than either Consciousness I or II people. He values the accessibility, naturalness, and nonpossessiveness of human relationships. He considers the degree of emotional intimacy present in one's life as the true measure of a man.

As Arthur Combs at the University of Florida has stated in many of his works, it is only as educational material at the intellectual level becomes personally meaningful in an emotional sense that it exerts an influence on personal behavior. If, for example, while writing letters at home in Los Angeles, you heard a news broadcaster state that a large American city was threatened by poisonous contaminants in its water system, you would probably say, "That's a shame" and continue your writing. When the reporter states that it is a large west coast city, you drop your task and turn the volume up. When he states it is Los Angeles, you will rush to family and friends with a warning, and probably go to a nearby store to purchase large quantities of other beverages. As the information, which was at first only intellectual fact, became gradually more directly related to your personal welfare, your behavior was influenced more drastically. So much educational effort is spent on memorization of facts (god word) not perceived as personally meaningful by the student. The very concept of memorization implies that the material involved is unrelated to self. Surely you wouldn't need to memorize that there was a dangerous situation regarding your water system. It mattered. You were influenced personally. In fact, you probably will *never* forget the experience.

To the extent you come to view emotional intimacy as a personal survival requirement, you will do something about developing it in your own life. As we address ourselves increasingly to emotional intimacy as a goal we will find new ways of relating to one another. Our individual and collective survival is at stake.

It is assumed that intellectual, physical, and emotional levels of intimacy are interrelated and that no one level is embraced to the exclusion of the others by fully functioning persons. However, it is felt that the evolvement and maintenance of emotional intimacy has been a relatively overlooked goal for most persons. Emotional intimacy is not a sentimental preoccupation, but is inextricably bound to the attainment of our survival goals in ways many of us have chosen to ignore.

In Part I we have (1) examined the need for intimacy from both psychological and sociological points of view; (2) suggested that the risks of intimacy are far less than the consequences of lack of intimacy; (3) explored the relationship between a person's life style of relating to the world and their view of intimacy; (4) pointed to some promising developments designed to encourage intimacy; and (5) explored the intimacy hierarchy.

The second part of this book presents, in a series of fable-like models, considerations of emotional intimacy which have application to human relationships from the two-person relationship to the global scale of the World Tribe—maybe ultimately to an interplanetary tribe. Regrettably, few of us now alive will be here to enjoy that exciting development.

part II
fables of our time

introduction

In order to bring to life the concepts in this book, a series of fables will be presented in Part II. It is hoped the models will provide a useful vehicle for organizing statements of commitment. "The Gospel According to Chicken Little" and "The Do-Gooder Syndrome" illustrate *causes* of a lack of emotional intimacy.

Harmful *results* of a lack of emotional intimacy are explored in "The Last One In The Box" and "The Lily Pad Theory."

"The Survival Manual: Bureaucratosophus Gigantus" illustrates some techniques for maintaining and enhancing emotional intimacy within a bureaucracy.

4

dangerous influences

gospel according to

chicken little

The fourth section of Part II describes Hope: New Ways of Looking in the "Declaration of Human Equality and Freedom" and "Conflict is Good."

Extensive research on those individuals who have exerted a negative influence upon the welfare of the human family reveals that one well-known personage stands out distinctively even when compared to Attila the Hun and the leaders of the military-business establishments during major wars.

The infamous character is none other than Chicken Little, the nursery story character who, after being hit on the head by a falling acorn, cried out, "The sky is falling!!!" and ran through the woods informing his friends of the imminent disaster.

One day, as Chicken Little was walking through the woods, an acorn fell on his head.

"Dear me," he thought, "the sky is falling. I must go and tell the king."

So Chicken Little hurried off to tell the king that the sky was falling. On his way he met Henny Penny and Cocky Locky.

"Where are you going, Chicken Little?" asked Henny Penny.

"The sky is falling and I am going to tell the king," said Chicken Little. "You come too."

So Henny Penny and Chicken Little and Cocky Locky hurried on together. Soon they met Drakey Lakey and others.

It seems that Chicken Little and his hysterical friends, including a couple of latecomers named Goosey Loosey and Turkey Lurkey, kept running through the forest shouting that the sky was falling until they encountered a cool, level-headed chap by the name of Foxy Loxy. Taking advantage of the general panic, he ate them all up.

The panic created by the forest colleagues resulted in their demise. They rushed headlong into frantic flight and were in the end consumed by their arch enemy, the fox. The improbable idea that the sky was falling seemed to gain favor among the characters in the tale as one after another they believed the story and added their voices in support of the contention.

Today's prophets of doom in the Chicken Little tradition are concerned with ecological disaster, population explosion disaster, youth revolution disaster, economic progress disaster, racial upheaval disaster, atomic annihilation disaster, and the imminence of moral decay.

The popularity of Chicken Little's dire warnings can be observed in many areas of human interaction. His message of darkness and doom, based on an unexamined assumption, is heeded by many members of the human family.

Many persons in psychological distress feel that improvement is unlikely and that, in the words of the public enemy propaganda artist, *the sky is falling*. They report, "I know it's hopeless!"

Students from kindergarten through graduate school who, as a matter of course, anticipate failure as highly probable and success as improbable are followers of Chicken Little's philosophy. "I'm only fourteen years old and it's all over!" Educators who feel that giving up restrictive and delimiting classroom practices would lead to sky-collapsing chaos are also believers.

Other disciples include: administrators who expect civil war with students; politicians who expect Viet Nam ad infinitum; segregationists who see integration as the end of the South and the beginning of mongrelization; and commentators who forecast the demise of America.

All persons who feel that man's nature needs to be controlled have, in part at least, embraced the chicken's message. His Gospel has been widely distributed and is often believed.

Who are the high priests of the Gospel according to Chicken Little? Unfortunately, educators, psychologists, statesmen, politicians, publishers, and parents often function as high priests by carefully teaching the Gospel to little people and adults. Its acceptance is a widespread as any other Gospel, religious or otherwise.

It is time the good chicken was laid to rest. Emotional bonds between men can create a new awareness of common ties and establish a milieu in which Chicken Little will be laughed at, not believed.

Do you believe the Gospel according to Chicken Little? Is the sky falling, or do you have an acorn problem?

do-gooder syndrome

There seem to be many educators, psychologists, counselors, parents, and teachers who travel through life wearing their respective social masks, but who are, in actuality, carriers of the "Do-Gooder Syndrome." This is an insidious, dangerous, chronic, and often terminal disease.

When students, clients, or friends come seeking aid for some emotional pain, helpers often resort to do-gooder techniques. They rush in to stop the pain by applying a verbal bandage: "You shouldn't feel that way! It will be better tomorrow!" They find it hard to simply be with the person without doing something to stop the hurt. The application of superficial cures—platitudes and truisms—often unwittingly communicates the idea that even in pain the client or student is incompetent and has no right to be in distress. This technique is damaging since it conveys little respect for the person in stress and is often founded upon the helper's discomfort at being close to conflict and unhappiness.

Theorists of existential-humanistic persuasions feel that the best help is given by someone who is simply there. Such behavior is profoundly influential but exceedingly rare. One counselor-educator stated that if he could do only one thing to advance the effectiveness of his counselors-in-training, he would sew their mouths shut to insure that they would listen to their clients and not offer do-gooder advice. This facetious statement makes a powerful point.

The helper's inability to refrain from applying cure-alls ultimately dehumanizes those persons who seek help. It would be more constructive to convey an active respect for pain. Such an acceptant mode is founded upon a deep conviction that only through fully and openly exploring the conflict in the context of emotional intimacy will the client or student be free to come to grips with it. *Being there, should be* the initial action; *doing something* can always come later! It is a matter of priorities.

Perhaps bandages, such as "There, there, Mommy will kiss it and make the hurt go away," should be discarded in favor of an application of emotional intimacy. Bandages cannot tie us together. They only increase emotional distance.

Are you a do-gooder in disguise? Do-gooders are found in many relationships: parent-child, clergyman-parishioner, counselor-client, husband-wife, and friend-friend. The Do-Gooder Syndrome can be hazardous to our individual and collective health!

5

outcomes of dangerous influences

the last one in the box

Species of laboratory animals differ from one another. Hamsters bite and are generally disagreeable. Mice also bite and fight among themselves. The lowly guinea pig, however, trusts. He docilely accepts his fate and seems to love his handlers as part of his basic nature. In some ways guinea pigs are more warm and "human" than some members of the human family.

A laboratory often has to kill guinea pigs in order that certain tissues or fluids can be obtained for research purposes. Fifteen or twenty guinea pigs are often brought into the laboratory in a box. As the pigs are removed one by one, one can imagine the frightened pigs remaining in the unfamiliar box saying, "Where is Agatha? She's been gone a long time!" "Herschel still isn't back!" "What are those frightening screaming sounds coming from the other side of the room?" "What will become of us?"

The guinea pigs crowd together in the box. They rub against one another to draw comfort and strength. The last two pigs huddle together as the group did. When, finally, only one pig remains, he is shaking, frightened, *biting*, and frantically nervous. He demonstrates many of the commonly agreed upon signs of severe psychological distress.

Humans, like guinea pigs, are often afraid of new environments, change, failure, illness, death. But humans have a unique tendency to define themselves as the "last one in the box." People often claim that no one understands them, no one cares; they are the last one in the box despite the several billion other humans who share the planetary box with them. They have sentenced themselves to solitary confinement.

First-year college students, lost in a new setting, often report feeling isolated and estranged. Reports of increased satisfaction in their new world seem directly related to the number and strength of ties they construct with others. Roommates, professors, janitors— anyone may become a tie, a hole in the box. They build a network of ties. Like a trampoline, such ties support them.

The following statements were obtained from three popular sorority girls who were teachers-in-training. These are only three of hundreds of such statements gathered from university students over the last two years.

I am the last one in the box every night about 3 a.m. I want to get out but I don't know where to go. I believed I was doing the right thing—now it all seems useless. There is nothing but my career and what's left of my family, but it's draining me. I left my husband because I was smothering with him. I wanted freedom. I wanted opportunity, identity. I wanted another man. Now all the things I trusted are deserting me. I'm confused. It wouldn't be right to save my marriage—the best we could hope for would be to grow old being content. Still the other man is driving me crazy—he loves me, but he's been hurt and won't trust not to be hurt again. The kids I hoped the most for are dropping out, crumbling, no one will listen or try to help me help them . . . I know this isn't hopeless or unique in my case, but it's eating me apart and I feel time is running out. I need an idea.

—W.

I guess the most recently I've felt totally alienated was last night. I live alone and for some reason I felt terribly alone. I usually enjoy my solitude but not last night. I wanted so badly to hear a human voice that I called 372-1411 and listened to a recording telling the time of day. It didn't help much.

—A.

Right now I am the only person in the box. There never was anyone else in the box with me. I have adjusted. At times I try to batter my walls down, or maybe fly over them into someone else's box, yet I never make it. I am always bounced roughly back into my own solitary confinement. My walls are clear. I see into the other boxes, they see into mine, but I am not able to communicate by speaking, seeing, or touching. I want to scream and say with my eyes, "I love you, everyone, you are beautiful. There are warm sparkles of sunshine everywhere, don't you feel them?" But my box includes my soul and it is frozen and I am alone. I walk alone, I think alone. I shall forever be alone.

—P.

A Nigerian studying at a large American metropolitan college set down the following poignant feelings upon his arrival in a new environment, away from family, friends, and a familiar culture. At the time of writing he knew no one in his new city.

TO A MIRROR

You lay your body bare
I gaze at you at will
There is none to call to share
to hold and spend this moment with
Oh, loneliness my faithful companion
In this strange world we are strangers all
How painful life can be!
Time it was when troops of friends
Cared to dine, to talk, and call
Alas, these are the days of the mirror . . .
—Kamaldeen Ibraheem

Each of us can recall a time when we felt like the last one in the box. It may have been an intense crisis situation or a situation which was similar in quality but less painful.

Recall some such experience in your life. What did you do that finally proved helpful? No doubt you tried many things before something happened, often almost by chance, which helped you get rolling again.

Results of research we are carrying on in this area indicate that the helpful event somehow involved another person or persons. It may have been a chance telephone call or contact with a stranger. Yet, the hole in your box most probably was a person. Not a book. Not introspection. Not self-discipline. A person.

Recently, suicide and crisis intervention centers have been set up in major cities throughout the country. A "hot line" phone at which someone is always available is a common feature: a permanent hole in the box of a person in need. The help offered to a suicide-prone person is similar in all these centers. First, physical survival is made certain. Then, all resources are marshalled to notify all persons significant to the person in crisis. Someone stays with him night and day. He is telephoned frequently and is virtually inundated with human ties, often somewhat against his wishes. In effect, the walls of his box are *battered down.* Only when the walls are destroyed do the crisis intervention professionals begin to feel that the crisis has begun to pass.

We all need constructive human ties. Tragically, we often take our individual boxes with us—to cocktail parties, marriage, or general human interaction.

The do-gooder approach to the dying person can have a dangerous, negative influence. Very often the patient is aware of his impending death and needs most to be protected from a lack of human ties. Because of their inability to deal with death and to continue to perceive the patient as "me," professional helpers, family members, and friends often treat the person as dead some time *before* death occurs. The patient wants to be fully included in the stream of life until the last moment. Yet, he is often the last one in the box. People speak in soft murmurs in the corner of his room and begin to humanly disengage from him during the very moments when he needs them the most. Medical professionals need to encourage the patient to share his feelings about his predicament. He needs to share himself, his feelings, as a way of avoiding the painful boxed-in feelings of isolation. To the degree that others box him in, he is being psychologically killed by those very persons who contend they are helping him in his time of need!

The last one in the box concept has application to the ways in which we handle aggressive behavior within our society. When someone misbehaved in the New England colonies, people said, "The devil made him do it!" Comedian Flip Wilson's similar line was a household word in early New England. Since the devil could be disguised as a friend, Puritans were skeptical of human ties. When someone misbehaves today we say, "The devil (bad environment, upbringing, alcohol) made him do it! He's just no good!" We then arrest him. If he persists, we sentence him to prison. If he still continues we give him the worst possible punishment within prison, solitary confinement. This is the most severe last one in the box situation imaginable.

This book suggests that aggression against persons arises as a consequence of a lack of constructive human ties. Yet, we deal with it by a progressive removal of ties instead of bending every effort to reconnect the offender with the human family. We may be handling such aggressive acts in the most ineffective way possible.

Being the last one in the box can kill us psychologically. The destructive feature of isolation is that we perceive *no* alternatives to it, no way out. Even though we know others are out there somewhere, we feel powerless to make contact with them. This is very different than being alone by choice when we know if we *wished* to we could enter into intimacy with others. Robinson Crusoe took his past with him and also had his man Friday. The Japanese soldier who recently emerged from his self-imposed isolation in the Pacific jungle and had been in hiding since World War II was physically alone, yet according to reports he was continually concerned about the war, his Emperor's situation, and the events that might follow his being discovered. He did, by his *own* choice, finally get out of his jungle box.

It is possible that emotional isolation and polarization resulting from defining ourselves or our group as the last one in the box has led and is currently leading us into all varieties of conflict with ourselves and one another.

As the World Tribe emerges, many feel the need is to develop skills in dealing with emotional intimacy. The current interest in encounter groups, Zen, drugs, and a process-oriented living can be viewed as outgrowths of that need. The emerging Person of Tomorrow, as described by Carl Rogers, demonstrates an increased skill in emotional intimacy in all of his relationships.

In our relationships with others, our actions can indicate "life" or "death" in much the same way the Romans did in the Circus Maximus. Death is signalled by boxing people in. Emotionally intimate relationships are votes for life. How do you vote?

lily-pad theory

A model is useful for setting up assumptions and exploring conditions related to them. For a discussion of our philosophical assumptions and our ties to them, we create a model in which existence is a pond of gelatin and each person lives on a lily pad in the pond.

Each lily pad represents the frame of reference or basic assumptions adopted by an individual to provide a modicum of stability. These pads have several important characteristics. The pads of the lilies are attached by stems to a common anchoring area, just as individuals are anchored to the human family by common needs. The length of the stem varies, however, allowing considerable difference in movement. The resiliency and stamina of the stems vary so that some pads can withstand natural stresses (such as visits by frogs and dragonflies) easier than others.

The flavor and nature of the gelatin are matters of personal perception. For most pad passengers, falling into the gelatin, into a chaotic situation, is a terrifying prospect. Such terror may spring in part from a lack of understanding about gelatin and its properties. Individuals have different specific gravities and a fall into the gelatin may result in different crises.

Two dimensions are important in lily pad theory. It is not only the pads or frames of reference that differ, but also the quality of the tie which the individuals have to their pads. A citizen of India has a pad that is quite different from a citizen of the United States. But the most important difference is not what beliefs the pads contain, but how the two persons view their pads.

Each person has a different view of the relative merits of his pad. Some have been convinced by powerful experiences that theirs is the only pad in the pond that can be effective in keeping people from drowning in the gelatin. Others are aware that their pad represents only one of the many possible ways of staying out of the gelatin and that there are more similarities than differences among pads. After all, the function of the pads is primarily to provide a means of stability and consistency.

A person's reaction to criticism of his pad will depend on whether he is rigid and defensive or flexible and secure. In response to a shout from the other side of the pond, "You are on the wrong pad" or more frightening, "Your lily pad is dying," the rigid and defensive person will attempt to obviate the criticism. If they cannot silence the voice, they will, in effect, "blow" its source out of the gelatin.

The exhortation "Don't make waves!" often comes from those pad passengers most precariously balanced.

Although humans delight in boasting of their information orientation in trivial matters such as placing a $2 bet on a pari-mutuel race, they seem to avoid at all costs any real examination of their lily pads. Human history of the fifty years since the "war to end all wars" in 1918 is full of examples of the application of the scientific, empirical method to all areas of human concern *except* lily pads (ideologies). Yet, it is this matter that is usually at the base when one human destroys another.

Holsti examined the content and quality of communiques issued by the six world power headquarters in Europe during the six weeks prior to the outbreak of hostilities in World War I. He found that as tension and dissonant input increased, an astounding psychological distance developed between the parties. Increased belligerence and stereotypy—repetition of the same posture—was evidenced by passengers of the six lily pads. Lack of communication preceded "blowing up" the other pads—an event we call World War I.

Other examples of intolerance of people's lily pads are found in history. The founding of the American colonies by the Puritans was not the result of their search for religious freedom as most elementary textbooks state. For the most part, the Puritans were tossed out of Holland and England because *they* were attempting to impose their views on everyone in sight.

Sixteenth century England was in transition. The security of the medieval world was breaking up as centralization of resources, national patriotism, and religious structures underwent alterations. Provincialism was on the decline. Following Martin Luther's challenge to the Roman Church in 1517 a period of ideological re-alignment continued in England during the 16th century. Catholicism, the Church of England, and various protestant groups were clamoring for loyalty. Puritans were Calvinist in temperament, seeking to purify religious processes in ways consistent with original scripture. They were strict in practice, intolerant in principle, austere in manner; they wanted to carry the Reformation to its completion.

According to Kai T. Erikson's comments on this period in his book, *Wayward Puritans*, the Puritan felt that "the Bible told him the difference between right and wrong, and in his efforts to shape the world to those clear moralities he could be positively ferocious." Puritan logic was not a method for learning the truth; it was a rhetorical means for communicating the truth to others. All important "oughts" and "shoulds" had been revealed once and for all in the Bible.

Max Weber, in *The Protestant Ethic and the Spirit of Capitalism*, discussed the Puritans' pride in their superior middle-class business morality which emphasized the role of the individual. Their refusal to co-operate with existing business and banking circles was the real reason for the persecution to which they were subjected.

Calvinistic thought held, on the one hand, that it is an absolute duty to consider oneself one of the elect chosen for "grace," and to exert all one's energy to combat doubts and temptations of the devil. On the other hand, in order to attain self-confidence concerning one's election to grace, intense worldly activity is recommended. Successful worldly activity was measured by wealth. Since Calvin himself stated that as few as one out of five believers might be chosen for grace, the spirit of aggressive capitalism gained impetus. Even the pragmatic Benjamin Franklin revealed his philosophic leanings in the money-saving advice in *Poor Richard's Almanac*.

We seem to be continuing the Puritan intolerance of other lily pads in this century. We have shown little understanding of dissenting groups within our social order. Current arguments remind us of the well-documented six-week period of stress preceding World War I. We see the Buckley's (conservatives) against the Vidals (liberals), poor against advantaged, students against administrators, and religious group against religious group.

Those of us who live in absolute certainty of our lily pad's contents not only feel the need to defend our unexamined position, but more tragically, feel guilty for even considering such an examination. When data appears that does not fit our frame of reference, we are uncomfortable and often distort or ignore certain portions of the data in order to resolve the conflict or avoid the pain associated with a forced examination of our pads. The implications for practitioners in the helping professions are obvious. A more open person reacts differently to criticism or new data. He realizes the lack of agreement with his present position and may comfortably examine another person's pad to see if elements of it could prove helpful. Such freedom of action is not available to those who are overly defensive.

Our inability to freely examine our pad can lead to many problems. Racism, one of our greatest social ills, is ultimately related to the lily pad theory.

There are two steps in racial persecution. The first step is to indict the victim group by identifying the issue with the group's name: Negro, Jewish, or Mexican. The second step is to heap blame for the society's problems on the victim group. The Jews were blamed for Germany's problems; the Negro was blamed for the problems in the South and later for crime in the northern cities; and some politicians now blame students for current American social ills.

Once these two steps are taken and no one challenges them, the final stage of the racist policy can be instituted. The Jews were executed; the Blacks were made second class citizens, and students are persecuted. Such irriational acts are quite consistent and follow inexorably once the unexamined premises in the first two steps are endorsed.

Children are often taught rigidity through religion, politics, or education. In Nazi Germany, for instance, young children were taught to read through captions: *Mein Fuhrer, Mein Fuhrer is gut!* There are people in the United States who feel we need to sell democracy with the same missionary zeal the Nazis and Communists use in promoting their ideology; we need to cultivate in youngsters an intelligent understanding of the meaning of democracy and an emotional attachment to its principles and practices.

The experience of American prisoners of war in Red China during the Korean War indicates that those people who are most open to the strengths and weaknesses of their own lily pad and those inhabited by others are best able to withstand pressures for conformity and capitulation.

In Korea those prisoners of war who were most easily "broken" were those who had been told only the merits of the American system and the negative aspects of Communism. One had only to shake their confidence in the American way through discussions of graft and insensitivity of the population to the war. After this, convincing these men that no one knew or cared whether they were alive or dead seemed sufficient to make them comply with the captor's wishes. Those prisoners, however, who were more widely informed about the strengths and weaknesses of American and Communist systems held up much better under pressures designed to break them psychologically.

The implication for education is that those students who are encouraged to be open lily pad passengers may be best able to cope effectively.

Open schools, patterned on British primary schools, are springing up in various parts of this country. These elementary schools are less institutionalized than traditional schools. They have old furniture, animals, and carpets which give a non-school atmosphere to the environment. Children are perceived by teachers and administrators as unique in their growth processes; they can proceed at their own rate. The teacher has much autonomy in curricular concerns. The emphasis is on concrete materials before abstract concepts. Evaluation techniques are informal. Children in such schools seem most accurately described as involved and happy. Intimacy among students, teachers, and administrators is encouraged.

The lily pad theory has something to say about change. If the temperature rises, and the gelatin begins to melt, the old frames of reference, or lily pads, may no longer serve their function; they may wither and die. It is doubtful that many of the lily pads that proved effective during the Middle Ages would be useful now. As mentioned earlier, our society is evidencing a rising temperature as the friction between various groups grows.

The survival of all may depend upon the willingness of pad passengers to cooperate intimately, perhaps by tying the pads together into a raft or by allowing pads to join and new pads to appear which will adapt successfully to changing conditions and will support older

pads. Such Darwinian adaptation may avert catastrophe resulting from future changes that cannot now be anticipated. It is well known that hybrids are often more hardy than pure strains.

Higher temperatures generated by activities within one or more pads may allow easier pad movement over the gelatin for both the generator and his neighbors. Certain pads can warm the gelatin around a neighbor and allow him to move if he so chooses. Such helping processes may allow pads to support an individual who has fallen into the gelatin so that he can again bring order out of chaos and begin to evolve a more effective pad.

The natural course of things can be figured out only up to a certain point and then only if we proceed humbly. If at any time we decide that our lily pad is perfectly correct, that we actually know "the truth," what the law of nature is, and therefore what is the right course of action, we shall find ourselves in the paradoxical situation of having to compel nature to submit to what we conceive to be its own laws! As we say, "Dammit! Why can't you agree with my lily pad?" In other words, it is only by doing violence to experience as we perceive it that the actual course of human and other physical events can be made to fit the oversimplified patterns in terms of which we attempt to describe it. Our lily pads often represent such oversimplified views. We become like Procrustes who streached or amputated visitors to fit his guest-room bed. Too much human energy goes into the defense of lily pads and not enough into their creative development.

The implementation of emotional intimacy advanced in this book is viewed as one relatively unexercised approach to dealing with the dangers of tragic polarizations. An attention to the common qualities of lily pads, their breeding and care, may be long overdue. It may be an overlooked survival technique that merits serious consideration.

survival manual

bureaucratosphus

gigantus

Persons often lament the damage done to them by large bureaucratic structures. All gigantic bureaucratic structures may be viewed as members of the species Bureaucratosophus Gigantus (BG). The species is similar in many ways to an animal kingdom species commonly termed elephant.

The BG is characterized by inertia, lethargy, absolute predictability, and structural transparency. All rules for its functioning are contained in published catalogs, organization flow charts, and staffing formulae.

The species, whether educational, military, or business, stays in its sleepy mode whenever persons around it are wearing proper BG trainer's uniforms and making appropriate BG noises. Such uniforms vary somewhat, but inappropriate attire rouses the beast to clumsy action, usually aimed at putting the situation back into an order conducive to sleep. Consequently, one sees successful students, faculty members, military men, and business executives displaying appropriate uniforms.

In universities, acceptable uniforms vary with areas of involvement. The faculty trainers dress conservatively if they are senior trainers (tenured), and more avant-garde if they are junior, (non-tenured). The trainers changeover can be noticed as trainers acquire tenure and status.

Among students (trainers-in-training), however, there are important differences in the uniforms. Crew cuts, white socks, and white shirts sometimes identify first term pre-medical, pre-dental, engineering, agriculture, and business students. Although dark socks replace light in a rather general way during the second quarter, other differences emerge. Science students dress conservatively and education students dress in slightly more daring styles. Political science majors shun crew cuts and begin to wear conservative flare trousers. Psychology and sociology majors emulate social action attire by wearing leather, long hair, moustaches, and flares. The most liberal seem to be drama and art majors whose dress is an expression of artistic freedom. It has been said that a coed can quickly guess the major of a young man by his BG uniform.

The BG noises, or vocabularies, also vary on a university campus. Students soon learn those noises that soothe the sleeping beast. The following examples reveal noises students find effective.

COLLEGE OF EDUCATION

"I have finally found my life's commitment (calling) —serving children. It is finally coming together for me."

ARTS AND SCIENCES

"Rigorous research and scholarship are my real interests. Education majors are less academically qualified than we, but someone must teach, I guess. The researcher is my hero."

GENERAL EDUCATION

"A broadly based program such as this, including Humanities, Sciences, and Language Arts is the only meaningful preparation for survival in the modern world. Who needs more technicians?"

MEDICINE AND NURSING

"Helping people is the only calling worthy of my real commitment. I will save the people."

These sample vocabularies can be heard in the respective colleges of any university. Stop and listen!! Such noises by students not only soothe the BG, but they also keep the trainers in that area happy.

It is curious to hear students, military men, and businessmen mourning their loss of freedom and opportunity for emotional intimacy when around this species. If, indeed, one elects to stay within the jurisdiction of such an organism, survival is readily accomplished. Anyone of average capacities can deal with this pathetic creature by giving only the briefest attention to published manuals (college catalogs) and minimal behavior requirements. After all, the BG is most characterized by sleeping behavior and transparency.

The violation of the training rules will arouse the BG to violent reaction and constant alertness to deviation. Neophytes to the world of the BG often tragically decide to launch an attack on the creature only to go down in glorious defeat. Any elephant trainer will tell you never to push from underneath the rear of an elephant. The results are often messy and tragic. Trainers, however, have learned to lead the beast while wearing appropriate uniforms and making soothing noises.

Warning: Aroused BG's may be hazardous to your present health and future prospects.

It *is* possible to evolve and maintain full intimacy while around the B.G. With an understanding of its nature, the task is not difficult. However, an examined approach is required in order to avoid the obvious barriers to intimacy which, by its very structure, the BG erects.

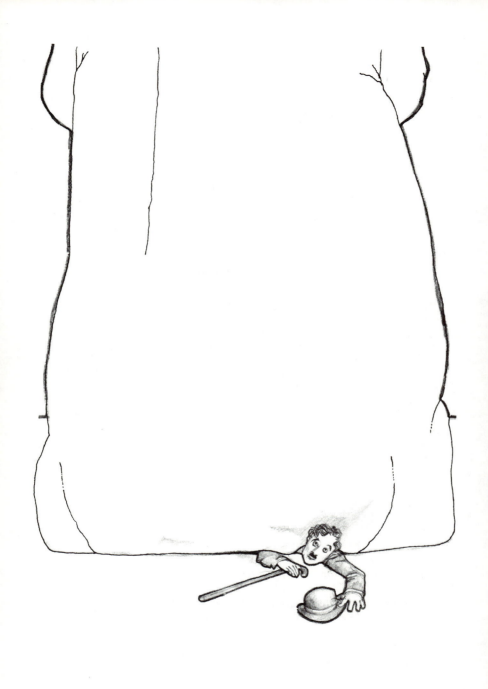

7

hope:

new ways of looking

declaration of equality

and freedom

Raising the issue of whether men are equal and free in the 1970s may strike the reader as untimely. Ever since the Declaration of Independence, which founded this republic almost 200 years ago, the question, "Are men equal and free?" has been continually examined.

James Madison and many others of his time, according to their writing in the Federalist Papers, felt that the unequal distribution of property in our society sprang from an original unequal distribution of talents. The aristocrat, Thomas Jefferson, incorporated such an assumption in his plan for American education. Jefferson thought that from the small township school the most gifted students would advance to the high schools. Again, the most gifted in the high schools would advance to the universities and colleges. We still embrace his view.

Psychologists and educators seem most vocal on the subject of human differences. The pioneering work of Alfred Binet and his associates in the Paris schools at the turn of the century focused upon the identification of those students unable to profit from traditional education. His pioneering work in intelligence testing has been expanded by current psychologists. Psychologists such as Anne Anastasi and Leona Tyler have written books exploring the ways humans differ from one another. Sex, race, intelligence, motor skills, and cultural heritage are discussed in their works.

In the face of work maintaining the importance of human differences, perhaps, after all, persons are equal and free in many more fundamental ways than they are different and the focus of attention needs to be changed. A change in emphasis to human similarities is long overdue.

All persons function within the limits of available time and energy and in any given time period the time factor at least is commonly enjoyed. Since individuals have a limited time to exist and can therefore not develop fully all of those talents they might wish to cultivate, men must select carefully from a multitude of possibilities those dimensions they wish to focus upon. The potential of mankind to develop numerous facets is relatively unlimited. Space travel, spectacular advances in medicine, and newly evolved social structures all testify to man's accomplishment of deeds formerly considered impossible. In hindsight, the present historical period will assume primitive characteristics.

Focusing upon one dimension diverts one's attention from others. Thus, a woman who writes a successful novel or earns $60,000 annually is concentrating on particular dimensions and may not have time to prepare excellent meals, marry, or rear children. There just isn't time for all. She has freed herself for achievement on certain dimensions by delimiting her exploration of others. The same reasoning would apply to loving mothers who might not have time to write several novels. Similar principles would help explain male differences.

To say that a person with highly developed verbal skills is more worthy than one with highly developed emotional intimacy skills is questionable. Such a statement does little more than reveal the frame of reference of the evaluator. In fact, psychologists often find that persons who have better verbal skills are often less able to honestly deal with emotion than those persons who have developed other dimensions of themselves.

Emotional health leads to an active selection of dimensions to be developed. Since persons seem to become their choices and their time for existence is limited, the choice of dimensions is vital. Assisting in this selection process may be a central role for parents, educators, and members of the society at large.

For illustration, two examples are diagrammed in Figure IV. Two persons, "A" and "B," have been diagrammed as having only four dimensions: creativity, emotional intimacy, earning power, and defense of self. It is apparent that "A" developed emotional intimacy and creativity more than "B" and that "B" developed defense of self more than "A." "A" is more creative and has less earning power than "B." "A" might be a creative artist or school dropout. "B" might be a businessman or college professor. Each might consider the other "less" if asked to make an evaluation. Yet, the total units of strength or capacity are equal—arbitrarily set at 100 units. The central consideration here is

FIGURE IV

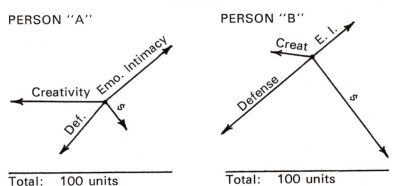

PERSON "A"   PERSON "B"

Total: 100 units   Total: 100 units

that different dimensions have been developed to different extents by the two persons during the limited time they have had. They are equal but different. One is not theoretically better than another. They are equal.

The introduction of a dimension such as defense of self perhaps helps to explain why some persons seem to fall short of the 100 units. Great amounts of their psychological, emotional, and physical resources may have been diverted to defend themselves psychologically. Since that dimension is not valued as much as achievement in our culture, the person is defined as less. In such a situation the best question may be, "I wonder why this person finds it necessary just now to expend so much time and energy in defense?"

People designated, according to our penchant for such categorization, as mentally retarded are a case in point. They are characterized by the quality of perserverance, especially in terms of human relationships. Often they develop capacities for human intimacy at the physical and emotional levels which make non-mentally retarded persons uncomfortable. The emotional intimacy dimension is not valued highly by most of society; yet for a variety of reasons the person limited in verbal skills has focused upon it. Such persons are not less. They simply have concentrated on a limited number of dimensions with their total units.

It is often stated today that traditional marriage is not for everyone. The idea of dimension preferences may help explain this. Suppose that a person has a 30-unit need for emotional intimacy. He will not have enough financial, physical, or emotional resources to develop a 30-unit relationship with 6 people. He may choose to enjoy 6 units with each of 5 people for the 30 total or 30 units with one person or some other combination. People simply have different preferences in this matter. The 30 units with one person seems to describe the traditional view of marriage. The 6 units with 5 people may describe life in a residential commune. To say that one arrangement must suit all is patently absurd.

Group marriage has a longer history than many people realize. It was discussed by Plato in *The Republic.* Communes of various types have been a part of the American scene since 1680. Many communes in the

United States today consist of monogamous couples. Group marriages are sometimes embraced in larger groups. Sexual relationships may be permanent or temporary. There are even single sex communes with and without homosexual activity. Many predominantly religious communes discourage sex except for reproductive purposes. According to Allen and Martin in their book, *Intimacy, Sensitivity, Sex and the Art of Love* the only thing that all communes seem to have in common is *happy* children!

Since people are not identical in their emotional make-up, different persons may embrace a variety of sexual life styles to meet their needs. Perhaps our social system has matured enough to allow persons to select their preferred distribution of intimacy units as long as no socially disruptive consequences follow. All may no longer be required to dance to the drumbeat of the socially endorsed "oughts" and "shoulds." The alternative may be social disruption. After all, most persons seem to eventually embrace a monogamous relationship, whether socially sanctioned or not, because of its deep life-sharing opportunities.

Devra Zinn, an American college student who has traveled back and forth for several years between this country and the Mishmar Hasharon Kibbutz in Israel, feels certain emotional advantages accrue to people reared in the Israeli communes.

Contrary to the popular belief, only 2% of the Israeli population lives on Kibbutzim. Kibbutzim range in size from 20 to 1,200 residents. The children born during a given year are reared in the Nursery until they are one year old. They then are moved as a group to the Baby House where they remain until age 4. From 4 to 6 years of age they live together in the Kindergarten House. They continue to move as a group through elementary and secondary educational levels. All classes are held on the kibbutz until the sixth grade; then students are sent to a kibbutz school in the nearest city.

Throughout the early years children are cared for by women assigned to the task. Parents visit freely when time permits. The educational experience is conspicuously free of individual isolation and competition is discouraged. There are no assigned grades. This is very dif-

ferent from the traditional American elementary and secondary educational process.

Although working and living
on a rural kibbutz necessitates the application of mutually
endorsed rules, all residents are encouraged to be open.
Acceptance of one another is paramount.

Development of capacity for
intellectual, physical, and emotional intimacy seems to be
encouraged. The children are happy, feel close to their parents, and retain strong feelings of identification with their
peers. The whole structure seems to encourage feelings of
belonging and worth for all residents.

A human being has more free-
dom in selecting his dimensions, both in the physical and
psychological sense, when he has more options and latitude in
his behavior. Psychological distress could be defined as a

FIGURE V
LIMITS: REAL OR IMAGINED?

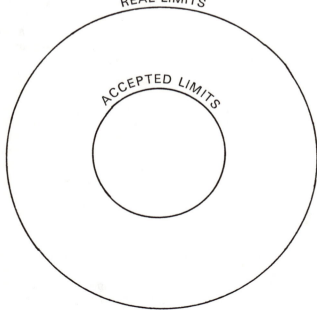

situation in which a person has no options and feels he "ought" or "should" do something that he prefers not to do.

Limiting influences springing from outside or inside a person may restrict the psychological degrees of freedom. The person whose functioning is inflexible is forced to display predetermined response patterns. Persons whose concept of self is negative and who see themselves as unable, unloving, unacceptable, and of little basic worth are also limited in degrees of freedom by these feelings.

Too little attention has been focused on the limitations that spring from inside a person while too much attention has been focused on the limitations emanating from external sources. External limits such as race, poverty, age, physical health, and family background receive an inordinate amount of attention from behavioral scientists. An emphasis upon the internal conditions necessary for freedom seems long overdue.

Not only do we define others as different, all too often we define ourselves that way also. We define one another as financially disadvantaged or advantaged, black or white, young or old, intelligent or dull, attractive or unattractive, acceptable or not acceptable.

Most people feel that they arrived on this planet as members of a particular family in a particular geographical setting with particular sets of physical characteristics, without being at all involved in the selection of those factors. We did not *apply* to be who we are. No one applied to be black or white, young or old, rich or poor. No child applied to be born in Biafra and become a victim of protein deficiency and die at the age of eleven. There are no applicants for crippling emotional illness or physical deformity. People are, in a very real sense, locked into a physical and cultural matrix. They must do their best to maximize their unique capacities.

The cartoon depicting two elderly people consoling each other that at least they *both* missed the sexual revolution makes the point. They would have enjoyed being young *now.* But, they were born in 1900. They did not apply for that year.

When citizens of the United States, a marvelously exciting young experiment in human social orders, regard themselves as superior, when Christians define themselves as "in the know," and when youth defines itself as "with it" to the exclusion of others because of a chance timing event in the course of the universe, the presumption involved is *staggering*, if not laughable.

A revolution would be effected in the quality of human relationships if each person viewed all members of the human family as engaged in the noble and brave effort to maintain what they are and to become more adequate and effective human beings. This human struggle is a profound common experience and each person attempts to achieve feelings of increased adequacy in the best way he knows. He tries the impossible. He dares to challenge arbitrarily imposed limits. When we do not apply our creative and critical thinking capacities because we think that we have no opportunity to do so, we may delimit personal growth. We may have a more active role than we dare hope. Assuming that arbitrarily adopted limits are real limits is dangerous. Tacit acceptance of our *only* tentative assumption about ourselves without testing it gets us into trouble.

The contribution that each can make to the other's struggle is to value one another's humanity and uniqueness and to free each other to grow. Ashley Montagu's definition of love as a mutual conferring of survival benefits speaks to this point.

If educators, psychologists, parents, and all members of the human family view one another in terms of our common humanity rather than our external limitations, many will redefine their roles and become more effective in their search for meaning and adequacy in their lives.

There is no reason why persons must be content with the usual limits. Perhaps, as Abraham Maslow and other writers indicate, most of us can reduce the time and energy expended on defense of self and become a 110-, 150-, or 200-unit individual.

How about you? Are you a passive pawn or an active origin in your dimension selection process? Are you actively functioning as an architect of what you will become?

conflict is good

The idea that conflict is good opposes the popular idea that if one is experiencing psychological or social conflict he should hurry to some helper, whether columnist or psychiatrist, to resolve the conflict and be returned to a mirror-lake tranquility.

Youth, aged persons, patients, and social planners often perceive dissonance as negative and feel that a "real" person of strength in the John Wayne tradition does not experience such discomfort. A more tragic and costly assumption could scarcely be imagined.

Henry Murray, an eminent psychologist, referred to the satisfaction resulting from the process of reducing tension. He discussed man's acceptance of challenge and his desire to try the impossible. Most people do not enjoy tranquillity and a lack of challenge. Once newly married couples have mastered the adjustment, they commonly look forward to the new tension-producing process of child-rearing. Recent graduates from college or university commonly talk of the need for new challenges often represented by graduate school. As a defense against boredom, retired persons often embark on new careers fraught with risk of failure. They do not want tranquillity.

O. J. Harvey's conceptual system theory (Part I) holds that conflict is a necessary condition of psychological growth toward more abstract levels of functioning, especially during critical stages of development.

The philosopher, Miguel de Unamuno, defined the human condition as "not knowing" the final answers to important life questions. He stated that our capacity to risk loving springs from our need for one another as we strive to bring meaning out of chaos. His book *The Tragic Sense of Life* written in 1921, is one of the finest statements of the results of conflict over basic questions.

There are certain "survival queries"—important questions that have no definite immutable answers—which must be constantly asked if one hopes to continually cope with a changing world. Examples are: What is the proper balance between freedom and control in a society? What is the proper role of education in a free society? What is the proper balance between law and order and freedom on our streets? These questions have working answers for a given time but must be re-answered as conditions change. The continual re-asking of the "survival queries" is a survival technique. If we allow ourselves to feel we have them answered once and for all, we are in trouble. We then pass legislation which is by definition unable to cope with the changing scene.

The myth of mirror-lake tranquillity is perpetuated in American society by a variety of spokesmen. Voices are raised opposing dissenting groups and theorists with new ideas. Therapists, social planners, politicians, professors, parents, and others continue to express the old conception that no "waves" is a desirable condition. This continues even when Americans seem to highly value violence in their entertainment pastimes.

Many parents, especially middle-class parents, mistakenly believe that love for their children should be expressed only through tender expressions of positive regard. The "oughts" and "shoulds" endorsed by such parents dictate that "good" parents are never angry and never lose their patience in front of their children. Consequently, they respond to stiuations that children *know* make the parents angry by demonstrating "flat affect." They are cool, unemotional, and nondemonstrative. Tragically, the child too often perceives this "flat affect" as a lack of emotional intimacy, as indifference to them. They feel rejected. Figure VI represents one conception of an emotional intimacy expression situation.

As the diagram indicates, caring is equally conveyed by tender and warm angry expressions. After all, someone must matter very much to us in order to make us angry. For a parent to hide the conflict because he has bought the tranquillity myth can be damaging to his children. If the parent wishes a relationship of real emotional intimacy with his child, he must dare to be himself, not the perfect parent as defined by others.

Dr. George R. Bach and Peter Wyden discuss the importance of the way in which warm

FIGURE VI

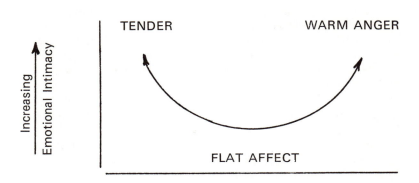

anger is expressed within intimate man-woman relationships in their book, *The Intimate Enemy: How to fight fair in love and marriage.* At their Institute of Group Psychotherapy in Beverly Hills, California, they have discovered that couples who fight properly stay together. Husbands and wives feel closer to one another when they have adopted standards of fair and dirty fighting in their relationship.

Constructive fighting makes for game-free living and a realization that intimacy is a process that requires attention—one of the central theses of this book. Conflict within a deep relationship can help facilitate the mutual process of growing together. Bach and Wyden even include information on how to score a fight between intimates and insure positive rather than negative long-range effects. They agree that conflict is good, even *necessary*, in the process of evolving true intimacy.

Human beings sometimes relate to each other as if they were square objects with sharp corners. The corners jab, stab, and scrape other persons; discordant relationships are the result. Whenever people are distressed, tired, threatened, irritated, or impatient they seem to show their square corners. The clashing of corners is expressed in emotional isolation, verbal or physical violence, or desertion of the field.

On the other hand, when humans do not feel threatened and are more accepting and caring they seem to become circles. Human interaction by circles is characterized by fewer discordant relationships, less dissonance, and by smooth contact of circle to circle. Common goals are pursued, sharing is encouraged, and basic trust is facilitated by the non-threatening, painless contact between persons.

The need for psychological conflict does not suggest that we relate only as squares. Our need for conflict is met in an internal, psychological sense. We need challenge. We need to emulate Don Quixote and live the impossible dream on our own terms as circles. Even Tolkien's Hobbits, who were gentle, "circular" creatures, experienced their share of conflict both within the group and with opposing groups.

Recent studies at the University of Florida indicate that persons found to be most open and healthy in their psychological functioning, those most self-actualized, have not enjoyed past life experiences free from conflict. On the contrary, their lives have held many painful, confusing, last one in the box experiences. Somehow, these people, when compared to others who are functioning less fully, have shown the capacity to use the conflict situations as rich growth experiences. In fact, less self-actualized people were found to show a lack of conflict situations in their pasts. Conflict is good.

In the Florida studies, people who were the healthiest seemed to be freer of the social "oughts" and "shoulds" than less healthy persons. They were more open to confusion and conflict and dealt with life's perplexities more openly with less need for defense of their lily pads.

Apparently, in a psychological sense, the human grows and becomes more adequate only when battering against the difficult. He often perceives emotional intimacy, productive work, loving, and good health as impossible goals. In order to find where the actual limits are, humans need to constantly test present limits. Many will find that they have grossly underestimated the degrees of freedom available to them.

Theorists point out that children in elementary levels should not be told that they are failures. It is appropriate for the child himself to discover that he is unable to do some things and needs to acquire more understanding. If some authority figure tells him he has failed, the child perceives himself as inadequate. Imposing such definitions is an insidious form of psychological homicide.

People who have bought the tranquillity myth often express a wish to return to a prior point in time in order to remake a decision. Such a return is really impossible when we consider probability theory in relation to perceptual psychology.

Consider figure VII.

When a person first considers various alternatives in a decision-making process, he considers the probabilities associated with success in the various choices (1).

Following his selection of one alternative (2), he immediately moves beyond the decision to a new area of vacillation and decision-making. Immediately upon his decision, all probabilities involved in the original decision change. He can never recapture them and remake his original decision in light of the old probabilities. It is impossible, for after pursuing the one course, he knows more about that alternative than he does about the other original choices.

His perceptual field has changed; he has changed. In a sense, he has become his choice. Thomas Wolfe in *Look Homeward Angel* and *You Can't Go Home Again* discussed the impossibility of regaining past situations. We can only go forward in dealing with the new probabilities at our disposal.

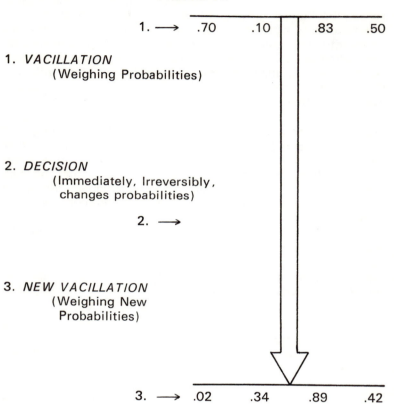

1. *VACILLATION*
   (Weighing Probabilities)

2. *DECISION*
   (Immediately, Irreversibly,
   changes probabilities)

3. *NEW VACILLATION*
   (Weighing New
   Probabilities)

Biochemically our bodies would like nothing more than to run back to an inorganic state of affairs, an absence of conflict. We call that condition death. Similarly, in a psychological sense, conflict is an absolute condition of existence. Perhaps capacities should be developed to effectively deal with conflict rather than expending so much energy trying to remove it.

The healthy person goes on to the next decision actively. The passive person bemoans his lot and wishes to do the impossible—to return to the original decision point and reclaim the old probabilities that are now irretrievable.

Conflict is good. How are your conflict handling capacities? Or have you bought the tranquillity myth?

part III
future course:
the practical problem
introduction

After looking at intimacy and its survival value in Part I, and the fables, which illustrate Part I's ideas in Part II, it is time to get practical.

In Part III, applications of emotional intimacy in particular areas of human interaction are presented. After spelling out the challenge before us and pointing to hopeful signs of an awakening commitment to emotional intimacy among youth and in educational, psychological, religious, and social action settings, I want to point out some of the *work* to be done. If we share the ideas in this book and nod our heads in agreement, but do not change the way we relate to our world, little of importance will have been accomplished.

Part III is a call to action. Perhaps we will be moved to do something about our commitment to each other's psychological lives through emotionally intimate relationships.

8

the challenge

If I am not for myself, who is for me?
If I am for myself only, what am I?
If not now, when? . . .

—*Talmudic Saying*

In the era of the emerging World Tribe, the capacity to evolve and maintain emotionally intimate relationships is a requirement for survival. Never before in human history have all residents of the planet found their future survival so inextricably intertwined with those of all other men.

While man's capabilities in science and technology are gaining control over environmental dangers, disease, and limitations of time and place, man's inability to maintain intimate ties has not decreased noticeably. This inability may have been bemoaned by clerics and poets in centuries past. Now it is the concern of all.

All we need to do is to convince ourselves that intimacy is a matter of survival and no doubt we will develop capacities for it. An organism that can conquer his environment for physical survival can certainly overcome past mis-education to free himself for psychological survival. The key is that he once *had* the capacity for emotional intimacy and later lost it. We have the potential; we need the inclination.

good-bye competition, hello intimacy

We must defy our Protestant Ethic and enter an age of cooperative, parallel human growth. We must become childlike and re-evaluate our well-learned inclination to classify others as "not-me" on the basis of superficial, meaningless characteristics. We cannot overlook the comments of Milgram, Speer, and Lorenz. Each in his own way contributes to our conviction that the moment we begin to see another as "not me" violence against that person is not only feasible, it is inevitable. Such violence may be subtle, like revoking student loans; or it may be active, like making war.

We may value the working man (the unsung hero) as much as the general. The poet as much as the engineer. The loving father as much as a head of state.

We need to move past intellectual distancing skills, to physical, and then to emotional intimacy skills.

psychologically defined good

An apropos characteristic of the fully-functioning human personality may be the capacity to say "I want" responsibly. The person is active. He is not a prisoner of externally imposed "oughts" and "shoulds." He has wants and shares them. Yet he says "I want" responsibly.

Responsible to whom, you say? To himself and others, of course!

Since he realizes the survival value of human relationships, he would no more violate them through destructive behavior than a window washer would cut his safety belt. The window washer would fall to his death. So would we if we cut our human relationships. Seen in this way the nature of our network of human relationships as a life support system acquires new significance. Since men need intimacy on some level, cutting off sources of intimacy for self and others through crimes against persons or things is a form of psychological suicide or homicide. Only severely disturbed people are suicide victims! When seen in this light the capacity to say "I want" responsibly, is a high-order, active functioning. It is not passive. It is not rigid and determined. Most important, it is directed toward mutual psychological good. In the final analysis, each person's irresponsibility comes at his own expense.

It is time those of us interested in survival took over from the death-dealers in our own areas of influence. Sometimes a kind word to a stranger is a vote for life. We each find many chances to vote for life or death in our own daily routines.

cybernetics

The term cybernetics, coined by the great interdisciplinary thinker, Norbert Wiener, was derived from the Greek word *kubernetes*, meaning *steersman* or *direction setter.* Although this concept has been mainly applied to science, computer technology, information processing, and related fields, the relevance of "system" input, processing, and output to human relationships is immediate.

A steersman in a boat must read wind direction and velocity, waves, tides, and stresses and strains within his craft. Similarly, each of us must read a variety of signs at each moment as to threats, needs, and available ways of finding the full life. We need to become active steersmen, architects of our own future, as members of the emerging World Tribe.

Throughout the last seventy years of American psychology, attempts have been successively launched, from different frames of reference, to understand just how, when, and why human organisms come to make certain responses to their worlds.

The work of Ivan Pavlov, which was later extended and modified by John Watson, Clark Hull, and B. F. Skinner, viewed the human organism as a system showing responses that were in some manner determined by a relationship between stimuli and response. Skinner chose to view the "connection" located between the response and the consequences of that response whether reward followed it or not. The emphasis on a type of connectionism was maintained, although altered, in his conceptualization. The steersman was given his orders by *external* conditions.

The pioneering work of Sigmund Freud in the early third of this century was extended and modified by his former students and later in turn by their colleagues and disciples. The emphasis in this view was upon the organism as a closed energy system striving to maintain balance among its components and to reduce tension.

Although Freud's point of view was concentrated on the internal dynamics unique to each individual, from one point of view, the old connectionist theories were still endorsed. The input stimuli were now conceptualized as internally derived, in the main, and the elicited response was viewed as determined by these stimuli, urges, tensions, and imbalances. The steersman was given his orders by *internal* conditions.

In recent developments pioneered by perceptual and humanistic-existential psychologists such as Rogers, Combs, and May, a more holistic, comprehensive approach to human behavior has been advanced. In this third force view, humans are seen as open systems and the steersman is viewed as having the capacity to opt for different courses.

Human behavior is best explained in this frame of reference as a product of an individual's perceptions of his world. Each person operates as steersman of his own situation and is much more influential in *changing* it than in the view of the behaviorist or psychoanalytic theory. He is not at the mercy of his past experiences of reinforcement or emotional traumas.

When he is not threatened, the individual is free to actively choose his responses to his world in ways consistent with his goals and aspirations. His primary motive is protecting, maintaining, and enhancing that person he now is and wishes to become. Consequently, the dynamic human system moving through time and space can be understood most adequately when attention is paid to values, life styles, human similarities, and the individual's search for meaning in life.

The modern motor car can be used as a model to assist in understanding the steersman concept. (It may be more familiar than the sailing craft.) In some ways human beings resemble motor cars moving at rapid speed through time and space. Both have a physical structure, internal processes, and a necessity for direction setting.

So often it seems that as a result of threat and well-learned passivity, the steersman in the careening human system is huddled in the back seat attempting to believe that the system is not in motion.

To encourage such a steersman to jump into the front seat to take command and to be an effective direction setter instantly seems most untenable. All of us profit from some basic instruction in the nature of the motor car, its power plant, its strengths and limits, and the relationship between controls and function before we can maneuver the machine.

Behavioral scientists should have already endorsed, in part at least, Jourard's position that the legitimate audience for information on the internal workings of man are men themselves, not the professional community alone. The situation now resembles a science-fiction tale in which psychologist auto mechanics refuse to tell drivers anything at all about the motor car. Some of the internal workings of the human organism have been discussed in this book in terms of the consequences of a lack of intimacy.

If we really endorse active steersmanship in a complex pre-21st century world, then each individual needs to understand as much as possible of the workings of his internal system. Physiology and some fields of behavioristic psychology are relevant here.

An appreciation of available control devices, brakes, warning lights, steering, and accelerator is also needed. Freudian psychology addressed itself to this need in terms of defense mechanisms, energy systems, and symptomatology.

Third force psychology, because of its assumptions of relative freedom on the part of the steersman, has rather uniquely addressed itself to the setting of direction, meaning, and values. The auto is not thought of as running on tracks like a train, but as being capable of travel on a variety of routes under a variety of conditions.

All frames of reference in psychology could be viewed as having much to offer to the understanding of the steersman role. Certain persuasions speak to different aspects of the vehicle's operation than others. To deny findings from whatever source seems self-defeating at best.

In a world perhaps best characterized by unpredictable rates of change, active steersmanship may be a matter of individual and collective survival. There is much to recommend a commitment to active steersmanship. We need to steer toward supportive human relationships in order to survive. If not, we may drive ourselves, quite literally, to death.

healthy persons

We need more healthy persons. The healthy person has a capacity for intimacy among several characteristics, most of which are at variance with our idea of the "well-behaved" person.

He cares for himself and realizes his uniqueness. He feels "enough" to cope with life and places highest priorities on human relationships.

He cares for others. He worries as long as one man is hungry or in need. He feels *personal* responsibility and sees all others as "me."

He lives in the *now* and realizes that life is made up of a series of *now* experiences. These are the "good old days" of tomorrow. He sees life as a now process.

He is spontaneous in expressing himself and abhors the hypocrisy so common at the strictly intellectual level of relating. Further, he does not find it necessary to label and stereotype. He can relate in authentic ways to persons, without categorizing them as black, rich, white, or authority figure. He shows an excitement at being alive and actively meets his world on his own terms.

These characteristics of the healthy person bear startling similarities to the characteristics of the effective helper as described by various researchers.

Many people would describe such a person as unstable, immature, not yet "grown up" (a synonym in our society for "grown dead"). Yet, he may be the emerging person who is more equipped to survive than "grown ups." He may be the model for tomorrow.

This healthy person would not believe in the Gospel According to Chicken Little, would not agree with the do-gooder, would be alarmed at the Last One In The Box and Lily Pad Theory, would subscribe to the Survival Manual, and would believe in the Declaration of Equality and Freedom, and Conflict is Good.

This composite healthy person is a goal for each of us. We will need each other's help through emotionally intimate relationships to move toward it.

9

encouraging signs

youth culture

The life style of many younger members of society includes signs of a commitment to emotional intimacy.

The tribal attire with its elaborate adornments can be seen as an expression of the celebration of life, an enjoyment of the "now." The folk rock musical *Hair* may be prophetic in its advancement of "being" in a role-free way as a highly desired value.

While its negative outcomes are deplored by all, the interest in the drug culture also may be an expression of a deeply felt need to belong. In the marijuana subculture many young people express the pleasure of feeling part of a warm, accepting, intimate group.

Works such as *The Last Whole Earth Catalog* (The 1972 National Book Award winner by Stewart Brand) are read by many people. This book includes a wide offering of books, gadgets, how-to-do-it instructions, and philosophical advice for those interested in dealing with survival, both physical and emotional, on their own terms. The introduction states that since big business, formal education, government, and church often leave little room for real human concerns, the catalog hopes to help return power to the individual to conduct his own education, find his own inspiration, shape his own environment, and communicate his experiences to anyone interested. The material includes explicit instructions for home birth, on the assumption that hospital delivery is not always "better." The noted anthropologist, Ashley Montagu, has argued this point for some time. He is fond of saying that hospitals are the very worst places to deliver children. Hospitals are the focal point of all the most serious diseases in the society. The ethic exposed by the popularity of *The Last Whole Earth Catalog* is one of questioning. Important, formerly sacred, assumptions are being challenged by youth.

The increasing interest in communal living arrangements, both rural and urban, is an expression of a need for more intimate interpersonal ties. Total immersion in a group seems to encourage the development of meaningful interpersonal ties.

Young people have embraced the helping ethic in the desire for emotional intimacy. They have expanded on the idea begun by the Peace Corps and Vista organizations and are volunteering their services in unprecedented numbers to projects from educational and social welfare organizations.

The revolution is a human one and in many ways younger people are pointing the way to meaningful styles of commitment.

education

Many voices are being heard within organized education calling for a humanization of the schools. Arthur Combs, Sidney Jourard, Charles Silberman, Neil Postman, John Holt, and others have clearly stated the need for humane educational environments in our society. The restrictive, authority-loaded nature of many educational atmospheres seems to resemble most closely the conditions in prisons and tragically traditional mental health settings.

Innovative programs such as the New School at the University of North Dakota, the New Elementary Program at the University of Florida, and the School of Education at the University of Massachusetts all are encouraging. These programs share a commitment to freeing approaches wherein the student-colleague is viewed as an equal, an emerging professional of unconditional dignity and worth. A common feature of these programs is immediate immersion of the students in a network of human relationships, both within the public schools and within his educational setting. Small groups are used extensively and students enjoy meaningful relationships with the faculty. Evaluation of progress is carried out by the student whenever possible or done cooperatively by students and faculty.

Indications are that students in such open programs tend to grow toward more healthy, less closed personality functioning and begin to see their role as that of freeing rather than controlling their future students within limits of responsibility. They come to value emotional intimacy as a high priority in a classroom atmosphere.

Research studies, discussed earlier, carried out in the College of Education in a large midwestern university indicated that the longer students had been enrolled, that is, as they moved from lower to upper class positions, the more they needed to be told what to do! Using the conceptual system constructs of Harvey, Schroder, and Hunt discussed earlier, we studied 633 students. The percentage of junior class members who strongly needed to be told what to do was 37 percent. This percentage increased to 44% in the senior class and to 69% at the graduate level! Although other variables, not related to education, no doubt influenced the dramatic increase, this traditionally structured college of education seemed to be accomplishing the opposite of survival education. A person defeats the purpose of education if he does not use himself as an "instrument" and feels the need to be given explicit directions in all matters.

The plea, "I was only following orders!" is an unacceptable rationale for a professional educator's behavior. This is the same plea advanced by Nazi war criminals and defendants in recent trials investigating military atrocities in Southeast Asia.

Indications are that the innovative programs in higher education will increase the openness of students. The graduates of these programs will function more fully, be more capable of surviving and passing on survival benefits than will graduates of more traditional programs.

The open and free school movements in elementary and secondary education are founded on commitments similar to those endorsed by university attempts at innovation. Students are encouraged to become active participants in their own growth. They play a large role, with parents and teachers, in evaluating their own educational progress.

Alan Gartner, Mary Kohler, and Frank Riessman in their book, *Children Teach Children*, discussed recent projects in which children taught their peers. They felt the benefits to the "teacher" were considerable. He seemed to learn how to organize material and gained deeper understanding as he attempted to master material well enough to effectively impart it to someone else. More importantly, a "tutorial community" encompassing the entire school often resulted. Such a community helps combat the feelings of isolation and uselessness that seizes children in our technological and urban society. These programs are increasing in number and may play an important role in the future. College and university students who act as tutors and counselors also seem to benefit. This movement to stress the helper-helpee relationship may counteract many last one in the box situations.

Programs at the urban-oriented Metropolitan State College in Denver are implementing the peer helper concept as a tool in helping educationally and culturally disadvantaged students achieve success in their learning environment. As an example, the Study Skills Laboratory of the Skills Reinforcement Center on campus uses some 60 student-tutors. Only 20 of these students are paid through the federally supported work-study program; the other 40 are volunteers.

The Study Skills Laboratory enjoys the cooperation of the Counseling Center, Financial Aids Office, academic departments, and faculty members. Attention is devoted to the improvement of reading and study skills, retention ability, and college adjustment through computer-based retrieval systems, taped lectures, sample examinations, and expert consultants in various areas of concern to the students. The real core of this program, which serves some 300 students each term, is comprised of the student-tutors. The student helpers often incorporate their laboratory involvement as part of their course work in educational psychology, sociology, and education.

Working on a 1 to 1 basis in a relaxed, informal physical setting, students help students. Initial indications of the program's impact are very encouraging. In this approach to learning, students who are receiving help relax and set about their tasks in a supportive human environment, an *intimate* environment. One tutor recently commented, "I think we are mainly involved in counteracting the negative influences of their public school experiences, and helping people they *can* succeed if they really want to!"

Each term over 70 students participate in a Psychology of the Helping Relationship course offered at Metropolitan State College in Denver. Students spend 2 hours in seminar meetings and 3 hours weekly functioning as helpers in various community agencies in the metropolitan area. They assist in methadone treatment programs for ex-heroin addicts, telephone "trouble" lines in crisis centers, tutorial programs, and community action programs. Overwhelming student response to this participation-oriented program demonstrates a desire to be the interface between academy and community. They feel such involvement is meaningful to them as they integrate academic work with their personal commitments. We are organizing a Center For Human Effectiveness at the college which will encompass a multifaceted approach to urban problems. Students plan to organize, administer, and staff their own community helping agencies as part of established course sequences.

A recent book entitled *Education And Ecstasy* suggests that educators will see education for emotional intimacy as a primary goal. Students will be helped to relearn capacities for emotional intimacy as they learn a new respect for feelings. They will learn the freedom of human expression in emotional relationships. Learning at the intellectual level will assume less importance and will be facilitated by televised instruction, programmed learning, and tutors in out-of-school settings.

Student personnel professionals in higher education, who are most concerned with out-of-class learning experiences, are also showing signs of renewed commitment to innovative approaches that move beyond purely intellectual levels. In the past, the professionals' contact with the student has been through counseling services, housing environment, or disciplinary action. Recently, however, most colleges and universities have included programs that meet students where they are in order to make services more accessible. Crisis "hot lines," drug abuse education programs, birth control information, and counselors are located in classroom buildings. This indicates to the student that the student personnel professionals are making every effort to combat alienation and to vote for life for their student colleagues.

In most institutions of higher education, students are used to help their colleagues in a variety of ways. They serve as resident hall advisors, lay counselors, drug education experts, and tutors. In this arrangement, the helper is often perceived as more accessible than the professionals in the more traditional "behind-the-desk" style. The peer helper concept is exciting. It makes the whole network of services more informal and casual; it becomes a routine rather than a crisis-to-crisis operation.

Educators at all levels are now seeing that psychological well-being and healthy personality functioning are important, indeed prerequisite, for successful academic performance. They are rolling up their sleeves to vote for psychological life.

psychology

Academic psychology is an arena of different points of view. The beginning student is often overwhelmed by so many different and useful schools of thought clamoring for his allegiance. The behavioristic emphasis is most entrenched and least assailable in terms of the body of knowledge accumulated. The adherence to data-gathering procedures acceptable to scholars in the natural sciences may, in large part, account for this.

Clinicians in the field of psychotherapy seem to be predominantly psychoanalytic in persuasion. They maintain a running battle with the behaviorists, whom they view as technocrats and reductionist dehumanizers.

A third force has emerged in American psychology in the last 20 years. This humanistic, perceptual, gestaltist point of view is, as implied earlier, very concerned with human dignity, worth, and the search for meaning in life.

Since the founding of the National Training Laboratories at Bethel, Maine, in the late 1940s a surge of interest in group processes has been noted in many settings. Many labels are applied to these group processes: T-group, encounter group, sensitivity group, and growth group.

My own experience and research has led me to a healthy skepticism about group processes. They have an exciting potential for assisting persons to develop a capacity for emotional intimacy when used by professionals who are aware of the limitations and hazards involved in such processes. Dangers include social coercion, inordinate dependency orientations, and painful experiences when "frailties" are exposed.

Effective group leaders are effective human beings who possess many of the qualities of the healthy personality discussed earlier. Their own personality is a much more important variable than any of the traditional considerations—method, technique, or psychological frame of reference.

The effective leader is free of the need to foster dependency and is well-grounded in his own philosophy of group processes. Such a philosophy often includes a commitment to emotional intimacy.

My own attempts have been directed toward removing the mystique from group operations and psychological help in general.

Most people who express a desire to participate in groups for personal growth wish to learn more authentic, role-free ways of relating to others and, more importantly, to regain contact with the person they *really are.* In short, they wish to unlearn their delimited style of relating to life and learn spontaneous, healthy ways to live in their world. But they also usually feel a deep ambivalence. They say, "I don't really know if I should participate." "It's probably just another fad." "Is something wrong with me because I feel the need to try this approach to growth?"

My approach to group work is that it is not mysterious; there is no hocus-pocus involved. Emotional work is involved, however, if growth is to occur. I call my groups "Tender Mutual Self-Exploration Groups" and view them as educational laboratories designed to assist in the development of emotional intimacy capacities. Every effort is made to expose participants early to the need for emotional intimacy.

Most prospective participants have tried other ways of growth, often including drugs, traditional psychotherapy, and much advice-seeking. They are now willing to try the group approach. My feeling is that emotional intimacy skills can best be learned in a context of human interaction, not introspection. Group processes seem ideally suited to this.

The group is *tender* in that the dignity and worth of all persons is an a priori assumption. No one need defend feelings or thoughts or submit to cross examination. Expressions of honest anger are, of course, encouraged, but not in ways that demean others. Feelings must be owned.

The process involves *mutual accessibility* in that the proceedings are carried on in group settings, not in isolation. Box walls are dissolved through mutual, tender, role-free interaction.

The focus is on exploration of *self*, not others. I feel that telling others what is wrong with them is such a well-learned skill for most of us that we need no practice at it. Rather, we need practice in self-exposure as we struggle for intimacy.

The group process is an *exploration* not unlike a safari into new areas. The truly noble and worthwhile adventure is to explore the human dimensions of self and others. The main requirements for success are courage and a commitment to the task.

The emphasis of the group is on process. As a leader, I "let it happen." The less verbal structuring, the better. Some persons seem to have embraced the John Wayne syndrome and feel that to share self is a "no-no." All members of the group are urged to express their feelings openly.

As an expression of my responsibility, I do spell out a minimal number of guidelines for the group:

1. No cross examination.
2. No physical violence.
3. No coercion to talk.
4. Feelings, not intellectual games, are the order of the day.
5. When members feel themselves leaving the group (psychologically), they have an obligation to other members of the group to express their "barrier feelings."

Productive groups move from intellectual to physical, and finally, to emotional intimacy along the intimacy hierarchy. (See Figure VIII.)

Initial attempts to sell the social self and share ideas on the intellectual level are common. Physical intimacy, broadly defined, is insured by the physical proximity of members. Hugging and touching is encouraged if members feel like doing so; at the same time they must respect the sacred dignity and worth of others.

As emotional intimacy develops, mutual accessibility, naturalness, nonpossessiveness, and process begin to emerge as dominant features. I am convinced that the development of a capacity for emotional intimacy can be as devoid of mystery as lifting weights to develop the muscles.

At the conclusion of a group, participants often report, "I never thought that I could be truly myself and still be liked!" "Others accepted me when I

FIGURE VIII

GROUP MOVEMENT MODEL

I N T I M A C Y

INTELLECTUAL	PHYSICAL	EMOTIONAL
words	touch	mutual accessibility
ideas	hug	naturalness
social selves	embrace	nonpossessiveness
games		commitment to process
distancing		

couldn't accept myself!" "I really hope now that I can batter my own box down in the future—besides, I know ways to stay out of boxes!" "Human relationships are the answer!"

The productive group process is not different in its dynamics from the effective 1 to 1 therapy session; but it has the same advantages as the peer approach in education.

Several psychiatric treatment centers, such as Fort Logan Mental Health Center near Denver, are applying group techniques to the treatment of emotionally disturbed patients. At Fort Logan milieu therapy is the focus. Patients, almost 90 percent of whom come only during the day, are part of a "team," an emotionally intimate community. The team is composed of a psychiatrist, psychologist, psychiatric social workers, nurses, mental health technicians, and patients. There are no uniforms (a "me-not me'' device) and informal first name relationships are the rule.

Patients participate in group therapy, play therapy, psychodrama, recreational therapy, and team conferences. Patient progress is determined cooperatively by staff and patients.

As growth occurs, patients relearn capacities for human relationships and regain capacities to cope with their own life situations, which formerly looked hopeless to them. With the permission of the team, patients spend fewer days per week at the center and subsequently participate in a variety of programs designed to assist them in rejoining the community as productive citizens. Arrangements are made to meet needs of individual patients.

Fort Logan and similar facilities represent one of the exciting enlightened approaches to the treatment of the emotionally disturbed.

religion

Organized religious institutions are in the midst of an agonizing reappraisal of their roles. Programs for youth, retreats for family groups, and more informal liturgical formats are seen everywhere. Although changes are fraught with trauma, the organizations *are* responding in important ways.

Community action centers sponsored by church groups in their *immediate* area are now commonplace. No longer are church members content to send missionaries ''over there'' to do good works. Increasingly, members themselves are getting involved in reaching out to their fellow men. They are voting for life.

social action programs

A variety of social action programs supported by both governmental and private resources are another promising sign.

Head Start, a program designed to help disenfranchised youngsters prepare for public school, and Upward Bound, designed to help disadvantaged high school students prepare for college, are examples of the expression of commitment to human equality.

The Model Cities program in metropolitan areas around the country is striving to improve housing, educational, and cultural conditions for minority group members.

Medical outreach programs, staffed by part-time volunteer medical professionals contribute to this thrust. At the University of North Carolina, the University of California, Berkeley, and at Harvard University, "people doctor" programs are preparing young physicians to deal constructively with the whole person—their medical, psychological, and sociological problems. Some medical school graduates are unhappy because earning power has become the sole criterion of success in medicine. They are personally reaching out.

There are important indications that governmental agencies, members of educational institutions, and concerned citizens are joining forces in a long overdue human liberation movement. This commitment to others is increasingly expressed from various sectors of our society as loud cries are being heard for a reshuffling of our present national priorities in favor of human resource programs.

10
call to action

The year 1969 marked the start of a new era of human life. When man reached the moon, Earth became an object of his detached scrutiny. This event precipitated an emotional breakthrough for humanity, for it ensured man's consciousness of his tribal intimacy as a species in the cosmos. Each of us can now know we are all in the same boat. We can envision a feeling of emotional solidarity with friend and foe alike. Explicit awareness of this intimacy among men and women of all races and cultures on Earth has become necessary for survival of our species. Technology has created the World Tribe for better or worse. Emotional collaboration is the only constructive possibility for the future development of human society.

This potential for emotional solidarity is both threatening and hopeful. All great changes in human consciousness have caused deep concern and anxiety. Modern technology, symbolized by space exploration, is now in orbit and ready to proceed to some prized destination. To succeed it must be directed by steersmen who are healthy, growth-motivated personalities. This book's thesis is that such personalities can only develop themselves in a constructive climate of emotional intimacy.

In order to achieve this constructive emotional climate, a vast transformation is well underway. This transformation is scientific, cultural, techno-logical, social, psychological, religious, philosophical, eco-nomic, and political. But the issue is still in doubt. Although promising developments can be found among youth and in educational, psychological, religious, and social welfare programs, many persons resist, often because they are de-liberately unaware of human ecological reality. Others resist because they are too intensely preoccupied with physical and economic survival. Still others because they are too profoundly conditioned by competitive existence to redirect their energies toward a collaboration consistent with the new human reality. This book is an attempt to facilitate constructive transforma-tions in persons who seek emotional self-realization for them-selves and other men and women. The essential nature of emotional intimacy seems clear.

Since this work is intended to be optimistic, pragmatic, critical, inspiring, and challenging to our closely held assumptions about human relationships, it is time to point out some of the work to be done as we fashion approaches to our individual and collective survival.

youth culture

As a result of the lowered voting age, young people may participate more fully in direct-ing our future course, and grow increasingly active in exerting influence on future developments. Since they have less un-learning to do they may be an invaluable source of survival advice.

The rapid assimilation of youth styles into mainstream culture will no doubt continue. As young people realize their voices are heard and their advice is attended to they will need to earnestly set about helping us get together.

Increased involvement in the formal and informal helping relationships through volunteer programs is extremely important. The establishment of out-reach programs apart from institutional settings is also needed. The youth-sponsored day care centers and free universities meet a real need in our society. More such programs should be organized.

Young people must stop "throwing themselves on the gears" and accept their share of the responsibility of insuring the physical and emotional survival of all men.

education

Educators are uncomfortable now. Those choosing to cling tenaciously to traditional views about the educational process are going to become much more uncomfortable.

Our society is taking a hard look at education, and healthy demands for accountability are being hurled at organized education. These demands will continue and increase in volume.

The once sacred bachelor's degree as a pass to certain employment is now suspect. With an oversupply of teachers, scientists, and Ph.D.'s, we are forced into a re-examination of education. What are its goals? What good is it? Should we follow the advice of the devil's advocate, Ivan Illich, and scrap the whole educational system and start over?

My feeling is that a serious attention to these questions will result in meaningful answers. Education may prove its usefulness by increasing the survival prospects of its students in the pre-21st century World Tribe.

As old assumptions are discarded, schools and colleges will probably move toward more open and less mysterious postures. No longer will the average age of college students be 20. Students of all ages, at all stages in their lives, from adolescence though old age, will enroll in educational programs to gain capacities for survival in a perplexing world. Ideas about evalaution, credit hours, course structures, and teacher-student relationships will change drastically. Educators will come to see themselves as liberators, not controllers. They will help people to be themselves so that students can use intellectual and creative capacities in more productive ways. That is what good teachers have always done.

If we examine the results of recent studies at the University of Florida and the University of Northern Colorado, we can no longer claim that we don't know what good teaching is. Students have always known. These studies have shown that if you ask students to name their best and poorest instructors, that is, those instructors who helped them grow and those who did not, there is surprising agreement among students. Although reasons for naming an instructor as good or poor differ, the agreement on which instructors are positive influences, effective helpers, remains.

Effective helpers are *not* distinguished from poor ones on the basis of the method or technique they use in classrooms. Whether they use traditional or modern methods is not critical. Whether they lead in their field in terms of vast amounts of knowledge doesn't seem to matter either, although minimal levels of competency are required.

The *perceptions* of the instructor are the crucial thing. His general perceptual organization, his perceptions of other people, of self, and of his professional task are the four variables which are critically important. The effective helper's characteristics are listed below:

GENERAL PERCEPTUAL ORGANIZATION

He tends to see people as more important than things. He is not mainly concerned with erasers, pencils, and the physical plant. His highest priorities involve human relationships; he values emotional intimacy.

He tends to see behavior of others as caused by here and now perceptions rather than by historical events in their lives. He focuses on the *now*. In many ways he fits the characteristics of the healthy personality.

PERCEPTIONS OF OTHER PEOPLE

He tends to view other people as basically able rather than as unable to meet the demands of their lives. Others are seen as trustworthy and dependable; more good than evil. He does not believe in the Gospel According to Chicken Little.

PERCEPTIONS OF SELF

The effective helper sees himself as adequate to meet the demands of his own life. He is not experiencing a last one in the box situation, for he feels he belongs in the world. He enjoys a feeling of closeness, for he sees himself as an attractive being.

PERCEPTIONS OF PROFESSIONAL TASK

The effective helper in various settings sees his task as one of freeing people rather than controlling them. He is not suffering from an advanced case of do-gooder syndrome. He encourages those he helps to open; he doesn't perceive his role as pushing people toward predefined goals.

It follows logically that since the effective helper is vitally committed to human values, sees others as able and trustworthy, and sees himself as adequate and valuable, that he would consequently see his task as one of freeing these worthy persons in the process of their own becoming. The growth emerges from the learner and is encouraged by powerful intellectual, physical, and emotional invitations from the effective helper. The Florida studies found this true of counselors, teachers, Episcopal priests, nurses, and college teachers.

It is time educators dropped their lily pad "holy wars" and proceeded with the work to be done. We need to use ourselves fully as innovative learners in education for survival. The development of the total, fully-functioning person is the common task of all of us. All disciplines and structures have something to contribute to the task at hand.

Let's cooperatively evolve some new lily pads as we free ourselves from past mislearning. It will be tragic if educators choose to remain in cloistered rooms intellectualizing about trivialities until the society at large thumps them into an awareness about the task before us. Some educators remind me of those threatened crew members who were frantically rearranging the deck chairs on the *Titanic* as it went down. Instead of such an absurd posture, we need to begin construction of a new craft which may be radically different from old structure in ways we cannot fully anticipate.

As Neil Postman and Charles Weingartner suggested in their book, *Teaching as a Subversive Activity*, the truly valuable educational process may become the examination of dangerous assumptions that are no longer of survival value. If we are not willing to discard false assumptions, Timothy Leary's dictum, "Tune in, turn on, drop out" may describe the course of events for increasing numbers of students. As they become aware of the meaningless nature of some aspects of organized education the students will drop out. After all, if the system is killing them, not to drop out is a form of suicide!

At the moment, many educators are in shock and much of the innovative educational thought is not being done by professional educators but by outsiders such as Erich Fromm, Edgar Friedenberg, Eric Hoffer, Marshall McLuhan, Alvin Toffler, and Buckminster Fuller. Fuller's book, *I Seem To Be A Verb*, coerces us to the realization that we are all in process; that is, if we are *alive.*

psychology

Within academic and applied psychology we must open ourselves to sharing our lily pads and evolving new ones. We must adopt positive facets of any and all views and create a new survival pad.

More outreach programs in the treatment of the emotionally handicapped are sorely needed. We can no longer overlook the tragic waste of human resources due to psychological problems. Low cost, effective mental health care centers, based perhaps on the best elements of innovations such as Fort Logan and on new ideas, are needed.

Psychotherapy is still a middle- and upper-class luxury. Its availability and accessibility must be extended through increased use of group processes and trained lay helpers who possess qualities of the effective helper.

In our society many people live lives best described by Thoreau: "quiet desperation."

Many executives, students, and working people who suffer alcoholism, heart attacks, stomach ulcers, and nervous breakdowns before being forced to stop to re-examine their "oughts" and "shoulds" are paying horrendous prices for their refusal to reassess their priorities. There can be no defense for such a requirement for receiving help. We need a more casual, accepted view of emotional help. It may come to be as accepted as visiting the dentist or physician for physical problems.

What is psychological help? A mere expressed desire to help someone else is not enough. Do-gooders do that. In John Steinbeck's story, *Sweet Thursday*, Hazel, attempting to help a wounded gull, chases it into the sea where it drowns. But Hazel meant well. We must create a well-defined goal for psychological help. That of increasing the needful person's survival prospects is one such important goal advanced by this book.

We will need to *make* all these changes.

religion

Organized religious organizations need to evolve new lily pads too. They should have more outreach programs. Relationships between the authority figures and the congregations should be more informal. There should be more appreciation for the human qualities we all possess.

This is a religious age. The increasing concern about meaning in life due to the rapid changes all about us is essentially a religious quest in the largest possible sense. Religious organizations need to join the stream and stop screaming, "Come back to our lily pads, you prodigals!"

The new interest in the occult and in Eastern philosophies with their passive emphasis is encouraging to me. Such interests are basically religious also. Religious institutions will need to abandon parts of their structure and organization to be acceptable to their followers.

The gap between verbal statements and practice must be narrowed. Important church leaders have been saying this for some time. Martin Buber, Paul Tillich, John A. T. Robinson, and others have joined the human quest by casting aside some of the "oughts" and "shoulds" of past assumptions.

social action programs

More and better social action programs are needed. National resource priorities must be re-oriented. The spending of vast sums of money to defend our foreign policy lily pad must be seriously questioned since our traditional foreign policy position was hammered out prior to the emergence of the World Tribe. It is no longer the United States of America (and some other people) on this planet. It is now a World Tribe that may eventually encompass the United States of Europe, United States of Africa, United States of Russia, United States of China, and United States of India. All will be equal members with us in the world family. What a shift in our view will be required if we are to adjust successfully!

Social action programs will give expression to an emerging emphasis on human values, not things. Youth, educators, psychologists, businessmen, churchmen, and politicians will join forces in pursuits vital to all—a recommitment to people. They may, for the first time, focus on similarities—not differences—in their goals.

11

conclusion

We have been maimed by our miseducation so that it is difficult for us to evolve emotional intimacy skills. Yet such skills may be a requirement for individual and collective survival. Either we begin working with each other for survival or our end will be soon. We need to rewrite the script. We need to be active architects of our future in order to ensure continuity for all men, not just the sociologically, educationally, or financially fortunate.

The key survival issue is one of degrees of freedom—options in our interpersonal relationships. The healthy personality is able to choose to be intimately involved or to be alone according to what he prefers at a given time. Process-oriented, fully-functioning persons have a variety of ways of relating in their repertory of behaviors. Emotionally intimate relationships are possible for them. Less healthy persons do not have such freedom of choice, for they are very often unable to function on anything other than the intellectual intimacy level. Capacities for genuine emotional intimacy must be increased as a requirement for full psychological health.

The need to live in a creative self-correcting process style is not newly observed. Buddhism has long held that men are often prisoners of *maya*, the "oughts" and "shoulds" advanced by social institutions.

Maya is perhaps most usefully defined as the sense-world of manifold phenomena, held in Vedanta to conceal the unity of absolute being. It is the reality of social order demands. One goal of students in this view is to cast loose from arbitrary *maya* and to enter the now. They hope to re-evaluate the insidious "not me" pressures and then opt to play the "game" or not. The breakthrough is a perceptual matter.

Alan Watts, a noted interpreter of Asian philosophy to Western readers, has suggested that Buddhists and Vedantists who understand their own doctrine profoundly do *not* believe in reincarnation in any literal, physical sense. In India, liberation went hand in hand with renunciation of caste. The individual ceased to identify himself in terms of his socially defined identity and role. The student was reincarnated in a perceptual sense. As he re-ordered his priorities, he truly became a different person in the here and now. He learned through his association with a guru (teacher) that much of the *maya* is illusion and is quite arbitrarily defined at his point in history by the institutional structures around him.

The guru refuses to give the answer, refuses to tell his student what to do. It takes great skill on the guru's part to help his student take over his own life, to be freed from well-learned "oughts" and "shoulds." The guru helps in a de-education process. The student comes to perceive his world anew in his own terms. In the words of a moving song, he is "free at last!"

The Christian concept of salvation, being "born again," bears striking similarity to the freeing experience within Buddhism. Being "born again" seems to be a perceptual matter also. It involves a reordering of human priorities which elevates love (emotional intimacy) for God and man as highest values. When a believer feels these priorities he is saved; he is a new person. He is free of this world's *maya* and reaches out to his fellow men. Like the guru's liberated student, the believer within the Christian tradition moves into a process mode of living.

The opening statements of clients entering psychotherapy resemble those of the guru's students. Clients hope that the therapist will tell them what to do and insist on such advice again and again. Most therapists are committed to *not* telling someone what to do. Gradually, reluctantly, clients begin to unlearn their belief that they are hopelessly caught in the *maya* of "oughts" and "shoulds" and start to take responsibility for their situation. They move from the position of, "I must do this," "I should do that," and "I ought to behave this way," to a realization that their *maya* is literally killing them. They tentatively explore disregarding the directives of others and discover like Chicken Little that the sky *doesn't* fall. They begin to live more openly, more adventurously. They begin to dare to become active. They become relatively "free at last!" They perceive their priorities differently. They may realize that the rugged individualism script is killing them. Relationships with spouses, children, lovers, and friends become more highly valued. Emotional intimacy is perceived as a requirement for life.

Students, too, often expect, because of their years of conditioning, to be told what to do by instructors. Tragically, many instructors feel that they have successfully met their obligations when they focus on this intellectual level. Truly effective instructors encourage full exploration of ideas and relationships. They do not value memorization—a practice that indicates that the material is not of immediate personal relevance to the learner.

Professionals in education, psychology, and other disciplines committed to encouraging healthy human functioning must come to see their role as liberators in the guru's and psychotherapist's style. No more imposition of "truths." Only a cooperative pursuit of tentative answers to the survival questions is worthy of our time and energy. As gurus for freedom, we must encourage people to become active, not passive. We must free them, not tell them, what to do.

A re-examination of "oughts" and "shoulds" is an immediate matter of survival for many. The corporate executive serves as one good example. He feels he "should" work 18 hours a day, be a successful drinker, play golf with the right people, be a good family man, eventually develop his own company, be a loner, and always appear supremely capable. He is caught in a "pipe" of often impossibly demanding, narrowly defined, "oughts" and "shoulds."

Many executives find that, in truth, their "pipe" is literally *killing* them, both emotionally and physically. They often say, supposedly in jest, "My work is killing me!" Yet they feel they dare not remove themselves from the "pipe" for fear of being labelled lazy, unambitious, or incapable. So, they go on until . . .

In our culture there are only a few socially acceptable ways to gain permission to leave the "pipe." Some of the most popular ways are nervous breakdowns, ulcerative colitis, bleeding ulcers, and heart attacks. Following one of these unfortunate "mishaps" those people around our executive give him permission to leave his old life style. They say, "Old Harold just was doing too much!" It's good he realized it in time!" Unfortunately, not all persons physically survive the frightful events in order to gain permission to leave the "pipe." What a horrendous price we often exact of others, and especially of ourselves, for our unwillingness to examine our "oughts" and "shoulds."

Once the premise that emotional intimacy is a requirement for survival is in part established, then certain institutions that legislate against it can be identified. Educational, governmental, medical, religious, and other institutions could be examined in terms of their encouragement of emotional intimacy deprivation.

The time for action is now!

What an exciting period in human history! Although we did not apply for this time and place for our existence, we are fortunate.

Many new and strange things are occurring. Some writers predict a workweek of 15 hours within 30 years. By then, educational structures may be unrecognizable. The measure of men may be on human dimensions, not material ones.

The concept of an international currency, a world medium of exchange, may hold much promise as a way to bring people together in a World Tribe.

An international language of some sort may be one way to encourage the development of emotional intimacy capacities on a global scale. It would at least help us get started on the intellectual level.

By the year 2000, it is entirely possible that the public will pay an admission price to enjoy an experience quite different from that available in a motion picture. By that time, the world may be so noisy and confusing that persons may choose to pay to sit and relax in a darkened theater and enjoy silence. Enterprising businessmen will no doubt offer a variety of environments for public enjoyment. Possibilities include the pounding surf, the open sea, a rainy day with thunderstorms, midnight forest noises, and many others. The latest technological methods of cinema and sound could be applied to provide this experience.

Man on the planet Earth is moving rapidly toward a global village. There have been three revolutions in the history of man. We are now in the midst of the fourth. The first revolution was the invention of speech in which man learned to communicate in verbal symbols. The second revolution was the invention of writing, not long before 3000 B.C. The third revolution—the printed word— occurred in the 15th century. The fourth revolution is upon us now and the first signs of its coming were included in the mid-19th century industrial revolution. We are in an electronic age of communication which is exerting as profound an influence upon us as did each of the preceding three revolutions.

This coming together will force man into the development of a collective survival ethic. This new event in the history of man may be intricately intertwined with the emerging concept of emotional intimacy.

As we develop fully we may need to go "out of our heads" to develop the capacities for full human functioning. We need to go beyond our cerebral *maya* and commit ourselves to deeper modes of living.

It seems to me that the most serious destructive human influences spring from reasoning based on faulty assumptions. Actions based on unexamined lily pads can lead us to so violate ourselves that we are physical and emotional wrecks at an early age. The cruel dehumanizing impact of actions directed toward others based on unexamined assumptions, as represented by racism, war, and repression, are much more pervasive than are crimes of passion. The latter incidents are usually restricted to small group or individual settings. The former can influence millions of people. The historical record of man's inhumanity to man during this century indicates that not having the courage to go "out of our heads" in order to freely examine our assumptions has been the cause of immeasurable human suffering.

There is a touching encounter in *The Little Prince* which shows the delicateness with which we need to handle our attempts to reach out to one another and how our "way" of reaching out ties in closely with the process of evolving emotionally intimate relationships. It also indicates how intellectual intimacy can get in our way.

> *(Little Prince): "What does that mean—'tame'?"*
> *(Fox): "It means to establish ties."*
> *"What must I do, to tame you?" asked the Little Prince.*
> *"You must be very patient," replied the Fox. "First you will sit down a little distance from me—like that—in the grass. I shall look at you from the corner of my eye, and you will say nothing. Words are the source of misunderstanding. But you will sit a little closer to me, everyday . . ."*
>
> *—de Saint-Exupery*

Yes, we must be patient, but we must try to get together and must begin to do so now. How to begin is the problem.

In response to discussions about the concept of full human intimacy—intellectual, physical, and emotional—persons say, "Tell me how to do it!" "Give me a checklist!" "Where do I begin?"

There is something profoundly repugnant about including still another list of "oughts" and "shoulds," in the tradition of the how-to-do-it manuals, in this book. In terms of the book, the assumption is that all persons have a capacity for intimacy, but have learned their limitations much as the Scarecrow, Cowardly Lion, and Tin Woodman did.

Perhaps the place to begin is to appoint ourselves as change agents in our own personal revolutions, to become freedom fighters for our own causes. As a beginning, since we know about intellectual—verbal intimacy (how else could we share these words?), we may want to turn our attentions to the physical and emotional levels. We might like to dare to try to defy those death-dealing "oughts" and "shoulds" founded on unexamined assumptions.

Dare to touch someone physically. A friend, a stranger, a spouse. This can be done even in the most casual situations such as conversations, luncheons, and business contacts. You will find that Chicken Little's sky *doesn't* fall!

In terms of emotional intimacy it might be fun to defy the John Wayne, Doris Day, Rock Hudson syndrome and try to do exactly the *opposite* of what we have been taught.

Offer *access* to others, in little ways at first, and then ever more deeply. Tell others where you really are and begin to accept their invitations to share their internal worlds with you.

Dare to try the impossible in terms of *naturalness.* Be yourself. Try it with others when you feel (Cowardly Lion?) that you haven't much to lose. The results could be amazing.

You may want to defy the talcum powder myth and begin to care for people quite apart from whether you will ever *possess* them in any sense. They will respond in ways that delight you.

Lastly, rethink your own priorities. If any part of this book struck a sympathetic chord in you, you may be at least slightly more committed to working at intimacy in terms of *process.* The real work to be done, of course, is to throw back those "oughts" and "shoulds" which will drive you away from others, not toward them.

How I wish that I were further along in this growth process that I could say I live this book's ideas fully and completely in my own life. I do not. These are goals for me. I grope toward them, but always fall short. I am weak and strong, distant and close, fearful and brave, warm and hostile, cold and loving. My progress is due to my efforts to grow, but mostly due to those persons with whom I've enjoyed brief glimpses of a real intimacy encompassing intellectual, physical, and emotional levels.

We seem to have embraced the myth that there is a scarcity of intimacy despite indications that over three billion persons share our predicament. When the intellectual intimacy "prophets" have us believing in the "myth of artificial scarcity" we settle for so much less than is available to us.

Since much we've been taught is working against us we feel great risk in embracing a new way of relating. I'm reminded of Machiavelli's observation that there is nothing more difficult to carry out, nor more doubtful of success, nor more dangerous to handle, than to initiate a new order of things.

There is nothing new in this book. But the survival requirement of the need to act on what we already know has a new intensity. Will we choose to survive or not? The ideas between these covers give just one of many possible frames of reference useful in making sense out of our situation. It is a call to action based on considerations emerging from many sources in our society. (Any pontifical overtones the reader may have noticed emerged from the sense of urgency about these matters which I personally feel.) How can we remain dispassionate about our own survival? I have tried to raise the issue of whether emotional intimacy is a requirement for individual and collective survival. If the question has moved you to rethink your human priorities as they are expressed in all your relationships, I am happy. Together we shall survive; separated we shall not.

It was not my intent to suggest that emotional intimacy is the only level worthy of our attention. On the contrary, full human intimacy is comprised of the dynamic, on-going interaction of intellectual, physical, and emotional levels. None should be neglected but none should be our sole concern. All levels are vital. Since we perhaps have most expertise at the intellectual level, less at the physical, and even less at the emotional level, considerable attention was devoted to discussions of the higher levels.

To some readers the thoughts in this book may seem contradictory. It was stated earlier that we are not now equipped to evolve full intimacy with others because of our past experiences. Later it was stated that there *are* ways available to establish intimate relationships.

What really has been done is to make a case for changing one of our most dearly held premises or assumptions, which, if changed, would revolutionize our ways of relating. The old and new situations are shown below in syllogistic form.

Old: If we embrace full intimacy with others, then we will be hurt.
We don't want to be hurt.
Therefore, we will not embrace intimacy with others.

New: If we refuse to embrace full intimacy with others, then we will psychologically or physically die.
We don't want to psychologically or physically die.
Therefore, we will embrace full intimacy with others.

Both hypothetical arguments, the old and the new, are examples of valid reasoning. However, the second is endorsed by this book and will carry us into very different ways of relating than the first. The re-examination of basic assumptions is a matter of survival!

My main regret at this point is that I am intimate only on the intellectual level, and then only in a one-way manner, with readers, and that I will enjoy the fruits of physical and emotional intimacy with so few of you. Perhaps the small and important human revolutions that will be caused in the arena of relationships by readers affected in some way by my ideas will sufficiently console me for not knowing you all.

I also regret that I needed to use an increasingly obsolete medium of communication, the printed word. Because the written word commands attention for only brief periods of time the ideas advanced in this book were assembled in the fewest pages possible.

Accept my warmest hope for a life full of the human riches associated with intellectual, physical, and emotional intimacy.

Become a part of the revolution in human relationships!

part IV
annotated bibliography

The bibliography has been divided into seven parts related to the contents of this book. A brief annotation of each reference is provided. The summaries should help direct persons desiring to do further reading to those sources most related to their particular interests.

This bibliography was selected from a vast number of sources relevant to the concepts discussed in the book. It is by no means exhaustive.

need for intimacy

Buber, M. *I-thou.* New York: Scribners Publishing Company, 1958. A foremost Jewish theologian and philosopher urges humane relationships. Instead of I-IT ("me-not me") relationships, the I-THOU relationships should be our model.

Camus, A. *The stranger.* New York: Vintage Books, 1946. A classic description of alienation and society's lack of tolerance for honesty.

Deviations from the *maya* of "oughts" and "shoulds" is dramatically punished. A central work in the philosophy of alienation by a Nobel-prize winning French existentialist.

Clark, R. *Crime in America.* New York: Simon & Schuster, 1970. A former attorney general of the United States criticizes our system of penology in this country. His recommendations for change, involving humanized approaches, have stirred great controversy. Dehumanizing procedures are decried.

Dreyfus, E. The search for intimacy. *Adolescence,* 1967, *2* (5), 25-40. Adolescent developmental crises are viewed as outgrowths of the search for emotional intimacy by the emerging adult.

Friedenberg, E. *The vanishing adolescent.* Boston: Beacon Press, 1964. The pressure of "oughts" and "shoulds" on adolescents is described. The time formerly allowed for exploration and play seems to be diminishing.

Fromm, E. *Escape from freedom.* New York: Rinehart & Company, 1941. The inability of men to constructively deal with freedom is examined by this classic work. Comparisons are drawn among medieval, early 20th century, and current societal situations. Common escapes from freedom through submission, destruction, and conformity are explored and a positive commitment to life through creative love and work is posited as a worthy goal. An active organism dealing with others in relationships of emotional intimacy is held up as a model. Relates nicely to *The True Believer*, conceptual system theory, and *Greening of America.*

Griffin, J. *Black like me.* New York: Signet Books, 1961. This moving work describes the consequences of dehumanization in terms of black-white relations. Mr. Griffin underwent chemical treatment and passed as a black during travels in the deep South. His reflections on his experience underscore the importance of the "me-not me" dimension.

Halsell, G. *Soul Sister.* Greenwich, Connecticut: Fawutt Publishing Company, 1969. The book, similar to *Black Like Me*, describes life as a black in contemporary society.

Harlow, H. F. and Harlow, M. K. Learning to love. *American Scientist,* 1966, *54*, 244-272. A summary of Harlow's studies of monkeys. Needs for warmth and mothering are explored. The after effects of maternal deprivation are discussed.

Hoffer, E. *The true believer.* New York: Mentor Books, 1958. The long-shoreman, self-educated philosopher points out the dangers associated with immersion in a cause as a source of feeling of identity. Closed lily pads are viewed as dangerous, for their "true believer" passengers see all others as "not me."

Holsti, O., North, R., and Brody, R. Perceptions and action in the 1914 crisis. In J. D. Singer (ed.), *Quantitative international politics: insights and evidence.* New York: Free Press, 1968. Pp. 123-158. The authors discuss the dynamics of a classic lily pad conflict: World War I.

Their findings are the result of creative data collection and analysis procedures using newest techniques.

Kanin, E. Sexually aggressive college males. *Journal of College Student Personnel*, 1971, *12*, 107-110. The study in this article suggests that the lack of emotional intimacy can result in aggressive acts against others.

Lorenz, K. *On aggression.* New York: Harcourt, Brace and World, 1966. A primary source on inter and intra species aggression written by a pioneer in such studies at the Max Planck Institute in West Germany.

Milgram, S. Behavioral study of obedience. *Journal of Abnormal and Social Psychology*, 1963, *67* (4), 371-378. A description of studies on obedience. Subjects were found to be astonishingly obedient in inflicting punishment on learner-victims through following the experimenter's instructions. Raises major questions about the role of obedience in modern society.

Miller, A. *Death of a salesman.* New York: The Viking Press, 1949. The story of Willy Loman. A poignant, sometimes humorous, ultimately tragic story of a man steeped in the go-getter gospel who never got beyond his own daydream. His moving struggle for feelings of human worth and acceptance is a central theme.

Robinson, J. *Honest to God.* Philadelphia: Westminster Press, 1963. The renegade Anglican Bishop posits a transparent honesty, especially about doubt, as a requirement for spiritual growth.

Spitz, R. A. Hospitalism: a follow-up report. In Eissler, R. S. *et al.* (eds.), *Psychoanalytic study of the child.* Vol. II. New York: International Universities Press, 1946. A report on studies investigating the influence of hospitalization on children. Youngsters deprived of human contact suffered both physical and mental effects which often continued for life.

Tillich, P. *The courage to be.* New Haven, Connecticut: Yale University Press, 1952. A protestant theologian explores the courageous nature of becoming. The risks of role-free, honest existence are spelled out.

Watts, A. *Does it matter?* New York: Pantheon Books, 1970. This book encourages a re-examination of the "oughts" and "shoulds" which seem to matter so very much to modern man. This book's ideas relate to *Future Shock, Bodies in Revolt,* and *Greening of America.*

fear of intimacy

Berne, E. *Games people play.* New York: Grove Press, Inc., 1964. The originator of transactional analysis describes the distancing games people employ to avoid emotional intimacy and how they can be unlearned through transactional analysis.

Chartham, R. *The Sensuous couple.* New York: Ballantine Books, 1971. This book even includes directions on undressing! It is not surprising to learn that the copyright on this work is owned by Penthouse International Ltd., which publishes *Penthouse*, a new men's magazine providing *Playboy* with competition.

Eisenstein, V. *Neurotic interaction in marriage.* New York: Basic Books, Inc., 1956. The difficulties associated with creating and maintaining an emotionally intimate relationship within a marriage relationship are discussed.

Ellis, A. *The American sexual tragedy.* New York: Twayne Books, Inc., 1954. The gamesmanship quality of American sexual encounters is explored. More honesty and less exploitation are urged.

Hodge, M. *Your fear of love.* New York: Dolphin Books, 1967. The risk of loving which acts as a barrier in human relationships is explored.

"J." *The sensuous woman.* New York: Dell Publishing Company, Inc., 1969. A how-to-do-it manual for physical intimacy. This book takes a plumbing, do-it-yourself approach. Although ostensibly written as a spoof, many readers take it seriously.

Jourard, S. *The transparent self.* New York: Von Nostrand, 1964. The need for interpersonal self-disclosure as a requirement for authentic human relationships is discussed. This leading humanistic theorist writes forcefully and views an emphasis upon physical and emotional intimacy as a requirement for survival. Intellectual intimacy is seen as a tool used in interpersonal distancing.

Kaiser, R. What happened to a teacher who touched kids. *Look*, July 10, 1971, 64-68. A description of the consequences of a charge of child molesting brought against a fourth grade teacher, Gerhard Braun (pseudonym). The emotionally charged events following the initiation of formal proceedings are recounted in detail.

Lehrman, N. Playboy interview: Germain Greer. *Playboy*, January, 1972, 61-82. The outspoken author of *The Female Eunuch* is interviewed by the Assistant Managing Editor of *Playboy*. With delightful incisiveness Greer criticizes the Playboy Philosophy, bunnies, and male chauvinism. A no-holds-barred, revealing interview.

Lowen, A. *The betrayal of the body.* New York: Collier Books, 1967. An examination of the schizoid personality. Physical symptoms of emotional conflicts are treated as a vehicle useful in reducing emotional difficulties.

"M." *The sensuous man.* New York: Dell Publishing Co., Inc., 1971. More "how-to-do-it," complete with exercises and a list of "oughts" and "shoulds" guaranteed to produce a superb lover even if he is short, bald, bow-legged, and a stutterer!

Menlo Park Police Department. *Interim-report—police uniform experiment.* Menlo Park, California: City, 1970. The results of a soft-look uniform experiment by a police department. Pre-experiment fears concerning safety, authority, identification, and durability were found to be unfounded. The soft-look uniform proved very effective even when formerly used measures of accomplishment were applied.

Moustakas, C. *Loneliness.* Englewood Cliffs, New Jersey: Prentice Hall, Inc., 1961. A classic description of the dynamics of isolation.

"P." *The sensuous child.* New York: Lyle Stuart, Inc., 1971. Allegedly written by a 13-year-old, this work is a "how-to-do-it" manual in physical intimacy directed toward the young reader. It is written in the "plumbing" tradition of *The Sensuous Woman, The Sensuous Man,* and *The Sensuous Couple.*

Powell, J. *Why am I afraid to tell you who I am?* Chicago: Peacock Books, 1969. This small paperback explores commonly accepted games, social masks, and other barriers to self-disclosure. Very readable and nontechnical.

Reich, W. *Listen little man.* New York: Noonday Press, 1948. This dynamic little book includes a heart-to-heart talk by the author to the "Little Man," the man trapped by societally taught "oughts" and "shoulds."

Shostrom, E. *Man, the manipulator.* New York: Bantam Books, 1968. The popularity of interpersonal manipulations rather than "being" in a process of self-actualization is explored in this readable paperback by an expert in psychological helping relationships.

Simons, S. and Reidy, J. *The risk of loving.* New York: Herder and Herder Inc., 1968. The fears associated with attempts to evolve intimacy are discussed. The need to take such risks is spelled out.

Watts, A. *The book.* New York: The Macmillan Company (Collier Books), 1967. This work discusses the ingrained taboo against really knowing who you are. Too many persons live lives of "oughts" and "shoulds" rather than saying *I* wan't!

experience of intimacy

Allen, G. and Martin C. *Intimacy, sensitivity, sex, and the art of love.* Chicago: Cowles Book Company, 1971. An intriguing discussion of ways to overcome barriers to full human intimacy on a physical level. Physical intimacy capacities are viewed as an important vehicle in achieving human closeness. Various scales useful in measuring your Intimacy Potential Quotient (IPQ) are included.

Allport, G. *Becoming.* New Haven, Connecticut: Yale University Press, 1955. A call to process living is issued by a foremost exponent of individualized psychology.

Bach, G. and Wyden, P. *The intimate enemy.* New York: Avon Books, 1968. The constructive management of hostility in intimate relationships as a vehicle for mutual growth is explored. Included are scoring charts for application in intimate fights.

Exupery, de S. *The little prince.* London: William Heeneman, 1964. A classic tale. The French existentialist aviator illustrates basic human needs for emotional intimacy through a beautiful child-like story.

Fromm, E. *The art of loving.* New York: Harper & Row, 1956. Emphases on the art of loving, an art that requires practice, are included in this popular book. Loving is seen as a process, not a goal which, once attained, lasts forever with no further effort required. Loving freely is a capacity that can be learned.

Hirsch, E. *The power to love.* New York: Alfred Knopf and Company, 1952. The dynamics of emotional intimacy and their application are spelled out.

Montagu, A. *The meaning of love.* New York: Julian Press, 1953. The human importance of love when freed from games is explored by the noted anthropologist who views a love relationship as a process which confers mutual survival benefits on persons involved. Such a definition is quite similar to that developed for emotional intimacy.

Morris, D. *Intimate behaviour.* New York: Random House, 1971. This new book by the author of *The Naked Ape* and *The Human Zoo* presents his argument that intimate behavior—and the absence of it—is central to our human existence. The famous zoologist describes and explains the necessity for the twelve stages that a man and woman pass through on their way to total sexual embrace. A revealing, in-depth look at the dynamics of physical intimacy.

Rimmer, R. *The Harrad experiment.* New York: Bantam Books, 1966. Rimmer describes a fictitious coeducational living arrangement involving intellectual, physical, and emotional intimacy at an eastern college. A thought-provoking paperback.

Segal, E. *Love story.* New York: Harper & Row, 1970. This poignant novel is a moving story of young love and the loss of an emotionally intimate relationship through the death of a spouse.

education and intimacy

Blume, R. Humanizing teacher education. *Phi Delta Kappan,* 1971, *52,* 411-415. A description of the emerging Florida New Elementary Program. The program incorporates processes and structures based on Third Force Theory in an attempt to encourage the development of open, creative elementary school teachers capable of encouraging emotional intimacy development in their classroom settings. A refreshing departure from traditional practices.

Combs, A. *The professional education of teachers.* Boston: Allyn & Bacon, 1965. Includes discussion of effective teaching from a perceptual-humanistic point of view by a leading theorist. A stimulating work.

Dahms, A. Educator's plea: I was only following orders. *Journal of Student Personnel Association for Teacher Education*, December, 1971, *10*, 2, 26-31. Attaining increasingly higher class levels—junior, senior, and then graduate—in a midwestern university's college of education was found to be associated with increased proportions of "tell me what to do" functioning by students. In terms of conceptual system theory, graduate students would be relatively less capable of flexibly adaptive functioning than juniors. Education may be "dangerous" in terms of future creative coping with perplexing problems.

Dahms, A. Preferred sources of help in time of crisis as related to conceptual systems of college students. (Doctoral dissertation, University of Northern Colorado) Ann Arbor, Michigan: University Microfilms, 1969, No. 69-15, 720. This study explored preferences for sources of help in times of personal crisis as related to the conceptual system constructs of Harvey, Schroder, and Hunt. System one subjects preferred authority figures, systems two and three subjects preferred peers, and system four subjects distributed their preferences freely across all sources. The study used 18,990 expressed preferences. Results confirmed predictions based on conceptual system theory.

Dahms, A. Teacher-counselor program in higher education. *Journal of College Student Personnel*, 1971, *12*, 116-119. A description of the University of Florida's teacher-counselor program. Instructors in a freshman course, Comprehensive Logic, also serve as academic advisors and accessible helpers to students during a 9-month course sequence.

Dahms, A. and Kinnick, B. Existentialism and student personnel work. *Journal of College Student Personnel*, 1969, *10*, 408-413. An interpretation of the existential mood in terms of the student personnel work profession. Ideas are traced from the 1800s to the present, drawing on Kierkegaard, Nietzsche, Jaspers, Heidegger, Sartre, Camus, Maslow, Allport, Rogers, and May. A discussion concerning human values and the helping relationship is included.

Farber, J. *The student as nigger.* New York: Pocket Books, 1970. An examination of the second-class status of today's student. The applications of arbitrary rules and demeaning sanctions are explored.

Gartner, A., Kohler, M., and Riessman, F. *Children teach children.* New York: Harper & Row, 1972. This work contends that although children learn from their peers, children learn *more* from *teaching* other children. Children themselves, through helping other children, learn how to learn and master subject matter understandings at deeper levels. The peer-helper concept may become an important element within newer educational structures.

Glasser, W. *Schools without failure.* New York: Harper & Row, 1969. This work indicts educational systems for their tendency to provide

students with failure experiences and urges a recommitment to success experiences. The developer of reality therapy takes a hard look at
education.

Kaplan, L. *Mental health and human relations in education.* New York:
Harper & Row, 1959. The potential positive and negative influences
of educational experiences are described. A stimulating book.

Kohl, H. *The open classroom.* New York: The New York Review, 1969.
The plea for more open structure in education based on personal
experience provides the focus of this book. Suggestions for change
and warnings about possible sources of resistance to that process are
pointed out.

Neill, A. *Freedom, not license.* New York: Hart Publishing Company,
Inc., 1966. In this book, the founder of Summerhill school in England
refutes his critics by spelling out his concept of freedom plus
responsibility.

Neill, A. *Summerhill,* New York: Hart Publishing Company, Inc., 1960.
The author describes a unique school in England which over several
decades has operated in ways very different than the traditional
American school. Freedom, not control, is paramount.

Purkey, W. *Self-concept and school achievement.* Englewood Cliffs, New
Jersey: Prentice Hall, Inc., 1970. An integration of research relating
self-concept and school achievement; this work urges increased attention to improving the self-concept as a central concern for educators.

Resnik, H. Promise of change in North Dakota. *Saturday Review,* 1971,
54 (16), 67-80. A description of the New School for Behavioral
Studies in Education at the University of North Dakota, Grand Forks.
This fluid, open approach to survival education, undertaken jointly by
faculty members, graduates, and undergraduates, bears striking
similarities to the Florida New Elementary Program. (Blume, 1971.)

Rogers, C. *Freedom to learn.* Columbus, Ohio: Charles E. Merrill Publishing Company, 1969. A thought-provoking indictment of present
educational structures. Results of research and recommendations for
action are included.

Postman, N. and Weingartner, C. *Teaching as a subversive activity.* New
York: Delacorte Press, 1969. A call to arms is issued to educators.
A call to overturn unexamined assumptions and educate for survival.
Practical guidelines are provided. Teaching is a subversive activity
when "sacred cows" are challenged.

Silberman, C. *Crisis in the classroom.* New York: Random House, 1970.
A write-up of the Carnegie Foundation studies in education chaired
by the author. A critique of present educational processes as responsible for grim, joyless atmospheres which harm children. Although the
original intent was to study colleges of education, the book focuses
on the public schools in the United States.

psychology and intimacy

Baum, L. *The wonderful wizard of oz.* Chicago: Reilly and Lee, Co., 1956. The delightful tale of the adventures of Dorothy, Toto, Scarecrow, Tin Woodman, and Cowardly Lion as each strives to have his wish granted by the Wizard of Oz. The movie version featured Judy Garland as Dorothy and Bert Lahr as the Cowardly Lion.

Blaine, G. and McArthur, C. *Emotional problems of the student.* New York: Anchor Books, 1966. The authors explore common emotional concerns of college students. The importance of isolation and reactions to loss of emotionally intimate relationships are examined.

Bugental, J. *The search for authenticity: An existential-analytic approach to psychotherapy.* New York: Holt, Rinehart, and Winston, 1965. The need for authentic, natural human relationships is discussed by a leading humanistic scholar.

Combs, A. (ed.) *Florida studies in the helping professions.* University of Florida Monographs, Social Sciences No. 37. Gainesville, Florida: University of Florida Press, 1969. A series of research studies on effective helpers using teachers, students, nurses, counselors, college professors, and Episcopal priests. Effective helpers were found to be identifiable not in terms of methods or techniques, but in terms of their *perceptions.* General perceptional organization and perception of self, others, and the professional task were all powerfully influential. Objectivity was found to correlate *negatively* with effective helping.

Combs, A. (ed.) *Perceiving, behaving, becoming.* Washington, D.C.: National Education Association, 1962. The 1962 Yearbook of the American Association for Curriculum Development (NEA) includes primary works by leading Third Force Theorists.

Combs, A., Avila, D., and Purkey, W. *Helping relationships.* Boston: Allyn & Bacon, Inc., 1971. This work applies theory and research in humanistic psychology to the helping relationship, broadly conceived.

Duncan, C. A comparison of certain experience by life stages of selected groups of self-actualized, modal, and low-functioning college students. Unpublished doctoral dissertation, University of Florida, 1970. An intriguing study that found self-actualizing subjects more like low-functioning than like modal subjects when total life experiences were considered! Self-actualizing subjects seemed to have *profited* from prior conflict in terms of more open functioning capacities. They transcended their difficulties.

Goble, F. *The third force.* New York: Grossman, 1970. A description of the emergence of the Third Force position in psychology with special attention on the work of Abraham Maslow.

Harvey, O., Schroder, H., and Hunt, D. *Conceptual systems and personality organization.* New York: John Wiley, 1961. The authors advance conceptual systems theory in this book. The importance of "ways of relating" or belief systems is spelled out. Many research studies are described and the relationship between conceptual systems and antecedent child-rearing experiences, attitude change, flexibility, and adaptation are described. The most open, least defensive system, Autonomous Interdependence, may be most able to create and maintain emotionally intimate relationships.

Jourard, S. *Disclosing man to himself.* Princeton, New Jersey: Van Nostrand Company, 1968. The book invites professional helpers to disclose themselves to men and men to themselves rather than remaining distant and "objectively" all knowing. A discussion of physical intimacy and scales, useful in measuring body accessibility, are included.

Jourard, S. (ed.) *To be or not to be . . . existential-psychological perspectives on the self.* University of Florida Monographs, Social Sciences No. 34. Gainesville, Florida: University of Florida Press, 1967. A collection of papers presented at the 1966 meetings of the American Psychological Association. Papers are included by Paul Pretzel, Kenneth Gergen, Sidney Jourard, Ted Landsman, and Herbert Otto exploring whether or not to be alive, a single self, transparent, one's best self, and self-actualizing. A stimulating little paperback for readers interested in learning more about the dynamics of the self from an existential-humanistic point of view.

Lindemann, E. Symptomatological management of acute grief. *American Journal of Psychiatry*, 1944, *101*, 141-148. The modal stages experienced when one handles the loss of an emotionally intimate relationship are discussed. The stages are: (1) emotional emancipation from dependence on deceased, (2) readjustment to an environment in which deceased is missing, and (3) formation of new and satisfying relationships.

Maslow, A. *Toward a psychology of being.* New York: Van Nostrand Company, Inc., 1962. A call for a psychology of process orientation rather than essentialist foundations is issued. Man's needs are placed in a hierarchy by Maslow.

May, R. (ed.) *Existence.* New York: Basic Books, Inc., 1958. A classic of extentialist writing in America, this book spells out assumptions of the existentialist view which are found to permeate much subsequent American theorizing.

Rank, O. *The trauma of birth.* New York: Harcourt, Brace and World, 1929. The theoretical exposition of "birth trauma" is introduced in the work by Rank. Much human behavior can be interpreted as attempts to return to the warm security of intra-uterine life.

Rogers, C. *Client-centered therapy.* Boston: Houghton Mifflin Company, 1951. This book first introduced the organized theoretical system of Dr. Carl Rogers to the broad professional community. It is still a valuable source of provocative and disturbing ideas.

Rogers, C. *On becoming a person.* Boston: Houghton Miffllin Company, 1961. A call-to-process living, a process of becoming, by a foremost spokesman for the Third Force position in psychology.

Watts, A. *Psychotherapy east and west.* New York: Pantheon Books, 1961. A comparison of Eastern and Western views on psychological helping and philosophy. Watts is a noted interpreter of Eastern philosophy to Western readers.

values and intimacy

Barnes, H. *An existentialist ethic.* New York: Alfred A. Knopf, Inc., 1967. A description of ethics from an existential point of view. Written by a noted existential scholar and translator of Sartre's works, this work refutes the contention that the existentialist view is, by definition, nihilistic.

Barnes, H. The ivory tower rebel and his philosophy. *Journal of National Association of Women Deans and Counselors*, 1965, *28*, 66-73. A call to a new appreciation of the dissenter's rationale is presented concisely.

Chenault, J. Help-giving and morality. *Personnel and Guidance Journal*, 1969, *48*, 89-96. The helper's responsibility attending the help-giving process is forcefully pointed out. Intentions in the tradition of the do-gooder are not enough.

Erikson, K. *Wayward Puritans.* New York: John Wiley and Sons, 1966. An interesting exploration of deviant behavior in general with special focus on the Puritan community in New England. Draws heavily on court records and original documents.

Frankl, V. *Man's search for meaning.* New York: Washington Square Press, 1963. Originally published as *From Death Camp to Existentialism*, this book recounts the author's experience in Nazi prison camps and advances his ideas of logotherapy. Psychotherapy is seen as first and foremost concerned with man's search for meaning in life.

Koestler, A. *The ghost in the machine.* New York: Macmillian Company, 1968. An able attack on behavioristic explanations of human behavior by a noted writer. Diametrically opposed to B. F. Skinner's *Beyond Freedom and Dignity.*

Polanyi, M. *Personal knowledge.* New York: Harper & Row, 1964. A philosopher of science points out the very personal nature of scientific inquiry. The myth of "objective science" is attacked.

Teilhard de Chardin, P. *The phenomenon of man.* (Bernard Wall, trans.) New York: Harper & Row, 1959. An existentialist writer explores man from a philosophic frame of reference.

Weaver, R. *The ethics of rhetoric.* Chicago: Henry Regney Co., 1965. An examination of rhetorical language—language that would persuade.

Includes an interesting discussion of the political usefulness of using ultimate, or naming, terms in rhetoric. Language used to move men to action seems to express or betray the ultimate values of its user.

Unamuno, de M. *Tragis sense of life.* New York: Dover Publications, 1954. Although written in 1921, this work by an outstanding Spanish man of letters and existential thinker describes man's struggles for meaning in life. The chapter on the practical problem of existence is an exciting statement of human commitment based on an ethic of not knowing the answers to major survival questions.

Weber, M. *The protestant ethic and the spirit of capitalism.* (T. Parsons, trans.) New York: Charles Scribner's Sons, 1958. Discussion of how the Protestant ethic founded on the thought of Calvin and Luther dramatically influenced the development of capitalistic business structures in the western world. The ethic demanded asceticism, hard work, and attention to Biblical admonitions.

view of future developments

Fuller, B. *Operating manual for spaceship earth.* New York: Pocket Books, 1969. Fuller, the exciting visionary of man's future, brings his creative genious to bear on major survival questions. There is no operating manual for spaceship earth. We need to *create* one based on examined human and technological understandings now available to us.

Hanna, T. *Bodies in revolt.* New York: Holt, Rinehart, & Winston, 1970. A philosopher looks at the present human dilemma in the face of a new world milieu. Now that technology has controlled the environment, men are turning their attention to human values. He identifies the proto-mutants who are the first signs of newly reordered human priorities emphasizing emotional intimacy. Related meaningfully to *Future Shock* and *Greening of America.*

McLuhan, M. *The medium is the massage.* New York: Bantam Books, 1967. The meduim or process of our time—electronic technology—is reshaping and restructuring patterns of social interdependence as well as aspects of our personal lives. Human relationships at all levels are influenced in important ways by communications media.

McLuhan, M. *Understanding media: the extensions of man.* New York: McGraw-Hill Book Company, 1964. The impact of modern media on man's life is explored by a leading communications theorist. The emerging World Tribe, based on an electronic revolution, is described.

Portola Institute. *The last whole earth catalog.* Menlo Park, California: Nowels Publications, 1971. A catalog of books, devices, food preparation hints, and philosophy which purports to help individuals assume control of their lives. It helps individuals assume real power in their struggles for existence without relying on government, big business, formal education, or church. An important book among those choosing alternative life styles.

Reich, C. *Greening of America.* New York: Random House, 1970. A discussion of three styles of consciousness and their emergence. The rugged individual of Consciousness I gave way to the corporate role-player of Consciousness II. Consciousness III is now upon us and is evidenced by new commitments to human values and emotional intimacy. A stimulating work.

Skinner, B. *Beyond freedom and dignity.* New York: Alfred Knopf, 1971. The science of human behavior is applied to man's present predicament. The concepts of human freedom and dignity are seen as mechanisms used to cover our lack of understanding of human behavior. A thoughtful application of human engineering techniques on society's development is posited as the means to human survival. A crisis solution is derived from behavioristic assumptions by the leading contemporary theorist of that school.

Skinner, B. *Walden two.* New York: Macmillan, 1962. This is a description of a utopian society founded on behaviorist principles. It was written immediately after World War II. It has been alleged that this fictitious account has been been extended into the real world of human events through the author's most recent book, *Beyond Freedom and Dignity.*

Toffler, A. *Future shock.* New York: Bantam Books, 1970. This best seller describes the increasingly rapid incursion of change on human life. Men are in shock and are unable to cope intelligently. A new commitment to accommodating change as a survival requirement is urged. Relates to *Teaching As A Subversive Activity, Bodies in Revolt,* and *Greening of America.*

Wiener, N. *The human use of human beings.* New York: Avon Books, 1967. The great interdisciplinary thinker describes the field of cybernetics and its potential influence on modern life in this book. The need to process ever-increasing amounts of complex data in order to cope effectively with existence is explained. The author explores the relationship between the quality of human life and modern technology. The need to evolve open, process-oriented lily pads is well-treated.

afterword

How I wish that I were further along in this growth process, that I could say I live this book's ideas fully and completely in my own life. I do not. These are goals for me. I grope toward them, but always fall short. I am weak and strong, distant and close, fearful and brave, warm and hostile, cold and loving. My progress is due to my efforts to grow, but mostly due to those persons with whom I've enjoyed brief glimpses of a real intimacy encompassing intellectual, physical, and emotional levels.

There is nothing new in this book. But the survival requirement of the need to act on what we already know has a new intensity. Will we choose to survive or not? The ideas between these covers give just one of many possible frames of reference useful in making sense out of our situation. It is a call to action based on considerations emerging from many sources in our society. (Any pontifical overtones the reader may have noticed emerged from the sense of urgency about these matters which I personally feel.) How can we remain dispassionate about our own survival?

I have tried to raise the issue of whether emotional intimacy is a requirement for individual and collective survival. If the question has moved you to rethink your human priorities as they are expressed in all your relationships, I am happy. Together we shall survive; separated we shall not.

It was not my intent to suggest that emotional intimacy is the only level worthy of our attention. On the contrary, full human intimacy is comprised of the dynamic, on-going interaction of intellectual, physical, and emotional levels. None should be neglected but none should be our sole concern. All levels are vital. Since we perhaps have most expertise at the intellectual level, less at the physical, and even less at the emotional level, considerable attention was devoted to discussions of the higher levels.

My main regret at this point is that I am intimate only on the intellectual level, and then only in a one-way manner, with readers, and that I will enjoy the fruits of physical and emotional intimacy with so few of you. Perhaps the small and important human revolutions that will be caused in the arena of relationships by readers affected in some way by my ideas will sufficiently console me for not knowing you all.

I also regret that I needed to use an increasingly obsolete medium of communication, the printed word. Because the written word commands attention for only brief periods of time the ideas advanced in this book were assembled in the fewest pages possible.

Accept my warmest hope for a life full of the human riches associated with intellectual, physical, and emotional intimacy.

Become a part of the revolution in human relationships!